The Wonder of Wool

A knitter's guide to pure breed sheep

Justine Lee & Jess Morency

DAVID & CHARLES
—PUBLISHING—

www.davidandcharles.com

Contents

Foreword 4
Introduction 6
A Brief History of Sheep 8
The Rise and Fall of British Wool 10
The Wonder of Wool 16
Choosing a New Direction 18

Breed Directory 20
Categorization: Old and New 22
The Primitive Breeds 24
    Black Welsh Mountain 24
    Boreray 25
    Castlemilk Moorit 26
    Hebridean 27
    Herdwick 28
    Jacob 29
    Manx Loaghtan 30
    North Ronaldsay 31
    Portland 32
    Soay 33
The Longwools 34
    Bluefaced Leicester 34
    Border Leicester 35
    British Milk Sheep 36
    Cotswold 37
    Greyface Dartmoor 38
    Leicester Longwool 39
    Masham 40
    Romney 41
    Teeswater 42
    Wensleydale 43

The Downs and Shortwools 44
    Cheviot 44
    Dorset Down 45
    Hampshire Down 46
    Llanwenog 47
    Lleyn 48
    Norfolk Horn 49
    Oxford Down 50
    Ryeland 51
    Shropshire 52
    South Down 53

Projects 54
Tools, Materials, and Sizing 56
Working with Heritage Wool 60

Furgus Unisex Jumper in Wensleydale Longwool 62
Cola Gilet in Leicester Longwool 68
Moina Sweater in Border Leicester 74
Carril Fair Isle Jumper in Bluefaced Leicester 84
Tara Cardigan in Castlemilk Moorit 92
Atha Checkered Hat in Jacob 100
Semo Sweater in Romney 106
Malvina Shawl in Portland 112
Orla Paisley Intarsia Sweater in Cheviot 120
Ullin Sweater in Black Welsh Mountain 128

Useful Information 134
Special Techniques 136
Sourcing Guide 140
About the Authors 142
Index 143

Soay	Devon Closewool	Lincolnshire Longwool	Northern Blackfaced	North Ronaldsay
Romney	Badger Faced Welsh Mountain	Dorset Horn	Herdwick	North Country Cheviot
Wiltshire Horn	Hill Radnor	Ryeland	Dorset Down	Greyface Dartmoor
Shetland	Shropshire	Cheviot	Hebridean	Kerry Hill
Clun Forest	Cotswold	Manx Loaghan	Exmoor Horn	South Wales Mountain
Suffolk	Oxford	Norfolk Horn	Hampshire Down	Castlemilk Moorit

Foreword

Wool is more than just a fibre – it is a living legacy, woven into the history of human civilization. For centuries, native sheep breeds have shaped landscapes, sustained communities, and provided warmth, durability, and beauty through their wool. Yet, in an era of mass production and commercial standardisation, many of these heritage breeds face an uncertain future.

The Wonder of Wool, celebrates not only the remarkable qualities of wool but also the critical importance of preserving the genetic diversity of native sheep breeds. Each breed has been uniquely shaped by its environment, developing characteristics that make its wool distinct – whether it's the soft and lofty fleece of the Romney, the hardy, weather-resistant wool of the Shetland, or the dense, insulating fibres of the Herdwick.

This diversity is not just a treasure of the past but a resource for the future, ensuring resilience in the face of climate change, disease, and shifting agricultural demands.

By safeguarding these genetic lines, we honour generations of shepherds who have nurtured them and ensure that future generations can continue to benefit from the rich variety of wools these sheep provide. The survival of native breeds is a testament to our commitment to sustainability, biodiversity, and the enduring wonder of wool.

Christopher Price,
Rare Breeds Survival Trust Chief Executive

Image: Dorset Down sheep at Rampisham Mill, Dorset.

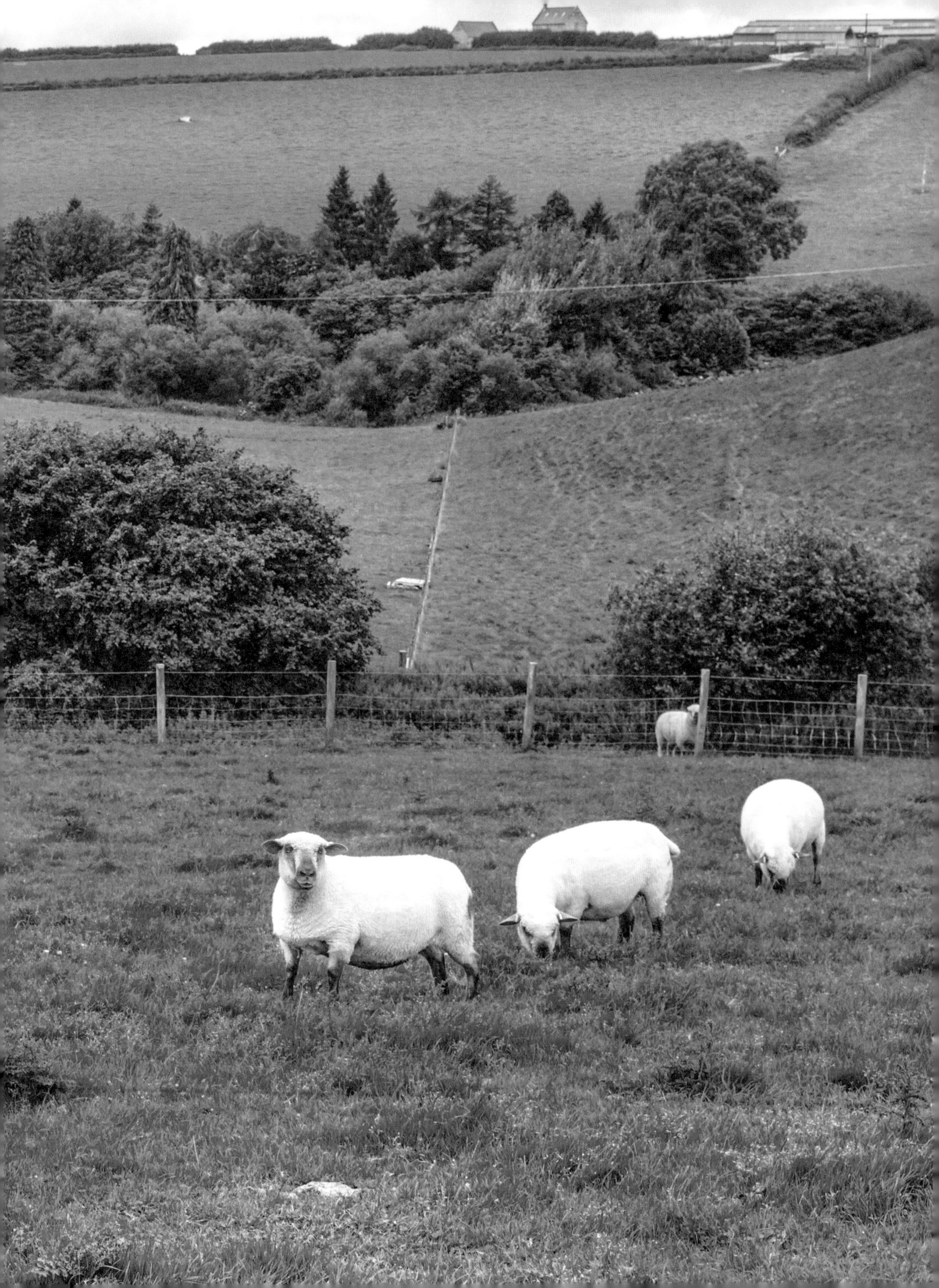

Introduction

For 30 years I have worked in the fashion industry, designing knitwear for some of Britain's best-known brands. It's a career that's brought me enormous pleasure: encapsulating changing trends; travelling the world to source new yarns; seeing a fashion company's rapid expansion, based on the success of designs we released with ever-increasing speed.

Then, in 2019, I picked up a book: *Fashionopolis: The Price of Fast Fashion* by Dana Thomas. And suddenly, for me, everything changed. I learned that 20 per cent of the 100 billion items of clothing produced each year go unsold; usually shredded, buried or incinerated. How around 9,500 garments are dumped into British landfill every five minutes, making textiles the country's fastest-growing waste stream.

I did more research, discovering that fashion is one of the world's top 10 most-polluting industries. Shoppers now buy five times more clothing than in 1980 and Britons buy more clothes than any other European country. I read how the explosion in cheap cashmere risks creating famine in Mongolia, where fertile land once used for human food is now pasture for goats. I wondered how I could have known so little about fashion's environmental impact, and decided to do something to redress this. So, 30 years after my first degree, I embarked on a Master's in Textile Design, focusing on creating a model for sustainable knitwear. A journey that would take me to every part of the British Isles.

When I worked as a knitwear designer, a key part of my job involved meeting agents. On a weekly basis I'd be shown ranges of new fibres and yarns – mostly sourced from Italy, Australia, or China. Occasionally someone would show me a British sample – just one weight of a dull cream wool that wasn't particularly soft yet had a price tag twice that of merino. Unsurprisingly I never once considered buying it. However, when I started looking into sustainable knitwear, local wool was the obvious place to begin. My first stop was British Wool: the organisation that represents British wool farmers. Anyone with four or more adult sheep is required to register and sell their fleeces through it, the only exception being Shetland producers.

Touring their wool grading and auction facilities, I discovered that Britain has 62 pure (or ancient) breeds of sheep, spanning a beautiful range of natural colours. Feeling the fleeces, I encountered incredible variety; some with much finer fibres than others. Yet at the time they were separated into just three grades: fine for apparel, medium for carpets, and coarse for insulation. These days, with buyers showing an increased interest in British wool, these grades have expanded. But still, if you want the softest wool, you have to be picky.

I knew this from four happy years spent at Ballantyne Cashmere. The fibre itself isn't damaging to the environment, particularly if produced in the way it was when Ballantyne still existed. Back then, limited numbers of goats were grazed only in the mountains of Mongolia where, because of the exceptionally cold nights, they grow a topcoat along with a particularly fine undercoat. When they moult in the spring, just one part of this (the underbelly) is combed out to source the softest hairs.

Running my fingers through the British fleeces got me thinking. What if there was a cashmere-equivalent sheep hiding here? Particularly if I separated out the best bits. I decided to knit a sample from all 62 breeds, experimenting with how well they knitted up. It took me a year to track down the wool or fleece for every sheep; grateful that each has its own breed society through which I could contact the relevant farmers. They all take huge pride in their flocks, yet few had ever been asked for a wool sample, especially for the purposes of knitting.

As the fleeces began to arrive, just as I had suspected, I found that some of the older native breeds – like the Soay and the Wiltshire – do have a soft, self-moulting undercoat. One dissertation and two years later I had completed my MA and reduced the 62 breeds to 12 I was confident could produce a yarn that was soft enough to knit and be a pleasure to wear. I'd also become self-employed, setting up a sustainable knitwear company called Ossian.

Britain has more breeds of sheep than any other country, with extraordinary lineages stretching back centuries. Yet our sheep farmers are in perpetual crisis. Business is jeopardized by cheap lamb imports, and wool is now so undervalued that shearing a sheep costs more than the price of its fleece. And yet the yarns produced from rare breed sheep are unmatched in terms of beauty, density, durability, and their range of natural colours. I am convinced that there is a sustainable knitwear industry to be fashioned out of heritage British wool. I am equally convinced that the fashion industry needs to find different ways of doing things. Urgently. This book is part of my mission to help find answers. "Too many clothes kill clothes", Jean Paul Gaultier once said. So we all need to buy less, but buy better. And yes, a hand-knitted 100 per cent British rare breed jumper won't be cheap. But nor should it be. It is, after all, a thing of pure beauty.

Justine Lee

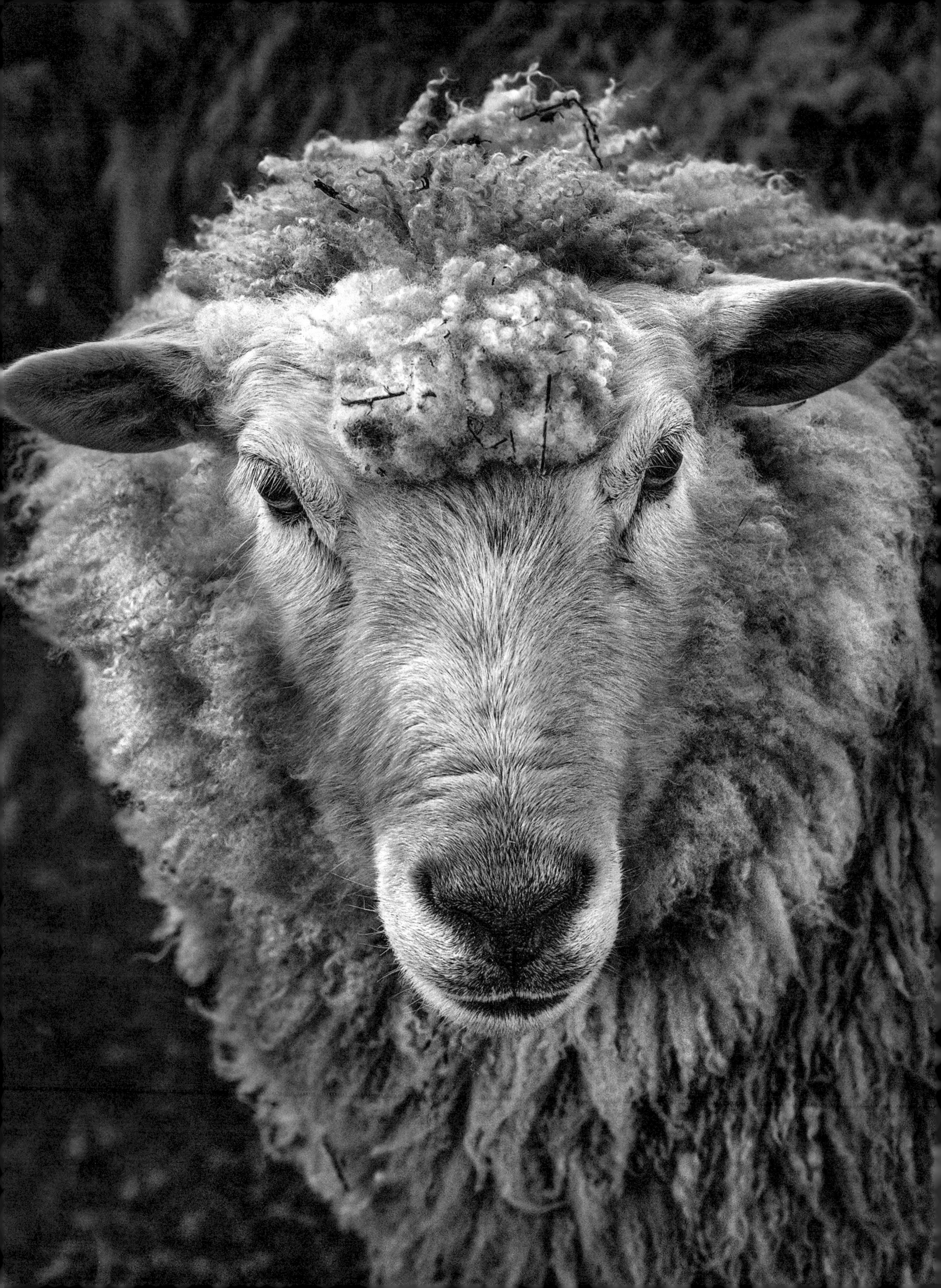

A Brief History of Sheep

Sheep have been woven into the fabric of human culture for thousands of years. Not only have they helped fertilize the land, provided us with food, kept us warm, furnished our homes and allowed us to create precious art, but they appear in myths, legends, and folklore.

Sheep Tales

The golden fleece of the winged ram – said to be a gift from the gods – is a central element in the Greek myth of Jason and the Argonauts, while in Egyptian mythology the ram represents creativity, rebirth, and fertility. (Here, we might pay homage to the real-life pharaoh Ramesses the Great, with his 100-plus children.) In Christianity, the "Lamb of God" is a title for Jesus, symbolizing his role as the innocent sacrificial lamb who takes away the sins of the world. In Irish folklore, sheep were often seen as magical creatures, representing a bridge between the human and mystical realms with the ability to see fairies and other spirits.

Sheep also appear in the Chinese zodiac (people born in that year are said to be gentle, compassionate, and artistic), and in Basque mythology the goddess Mari was said to live in a cave with her flock, bringing prosperity to those who respected her. Ethiopian and Somali folklore tells of a golden sheep whose wool also brought prosperity to its owners. Although the stories also include themes of greed and the consequences of exploiting nature for personal gain. In Bedouin folklore, wise shepherds use their knowledge and intuition to protect their flocks from harm, while a shepherd's search for his sheep represents the human soul's journey towards enlightenment.

One of the most significant legends involving sheep in the Islamic tradition is that of the Prophet Ibrahim (Abraham) and his willingness to sacrifice his son Ishmael as an act of obedience to God. At the last moment, God provides a ram to be sacrificed instead. The event is commemorated during Eid al-Adha, the Festival of Sacrifice, where sheep (or other livestock) are slaughtered in remembrance of Ibrahim's faith and obedience.

In some cultures, the behaviour of sheep is used to predict weather changes. For example, if they're seen huddling closely together it's said that there's a storm approaching. There's also an Australian nursery that advocates burying a sheep's liver a spade's depth under your passion fruit – probably because the liver is high in iron, and over time provides rich nutrients for the hungry vine.

Sheep before Shepherds

Between 10 and 20 million years ago, an animal called the mouflon wandered the freezing mountains of central Asia. With a robust body and looking as much like a goat as a sheep, it had large horns, a coarse dark coat, and a soft, woolly undercoat that naturally moulted annually.

The mouflon is the breed from which all modern sheep originate. Today the European mouflon still survives in pockets of Sardinia, Corsica, and Cyprus, but its Asiatic ancestor has long been lost through cross-breeding.

Selective breeding has also been carried out for millennia. Early farmers would have selected certain characteristics such as submissiveness, thus making their sheep easier to control. Equally, sheep with thick, soft wool would have been prioritized. Meanwhile, those with high levels of aggression would have been killed – along with others that had horns or were too large to handle.

This breeding for docility is one of the reasons why sheep have gained their reputation for stupidity – something that's simply not true. Academic studies show that they can recognize and remember at least 50 different faces for up to two years, and Cambridge University scientists found that they rivalled monkeys and humans in certain learning tasks. Meanwhile, a report published by Animal Welfare found that sheep are capable of experiencing a whole range of feelings: despair, boredom, and happiness, as well as fear.

Sheep on a Roll

In 2004 it was reported across the British media that the local people of Marsden in West Yorkshire had solved the mystery of how sheep from the surrounding moors continued to invade the small town. Despite cattle grids having been installed on the perimeter, the sheep kept raiding the town's gardens, cricket pitch, bowling green, and graveyards, eating flowers, plants, and vegetables. It turned out that the crafty flock had taught themselves to roll over the 3m (10ft) cattle grids, lying on their sides or backs and rolling over and over the bars until they cleared them. Rather like SAS commandoes.

Bringing Sheep in from the Wild

Around 11,000 years ago our hunter-gatherer ancestors had become less nomadic and were cultivating crops and rearing domestic animals – including sheep. Domesticated sheep would have provided milk, cheese, lanolin, sheepskins, wool, and fertilizer, so were a vital part of human development.

The area that is now Iran was at the heart of sheep domestication. Well-preserved scraps of woollen textiles, showing eight different types of fleece and dated as being about 5,000 years old, were found in eastern Iran, near the Afghanistan border. Ancient Iraqi records from the end of the third millennium BCE describe at least five categories of wool, and we know that shepherds would have been controlling vast flocks, some numbering as many as 27,000 sheep.

In Britain, the first recorded sheep appear around the same time, having arrived during the Neolithic period. Also looking more like goats, these small, wiry creatures bear a genetic make-up close to the Soay sheep, still found in the St Kilda archipelago off the coast of Scotland. Once described as living fossils, the Soay gained its name from the Old Norse word "Sauðey", meaning island of sheep.

While wild sheep used to naturally shed their fleeces (and some ancient breeds still do) domesticated ones had this trait bred out of them – although ironically some farmers are now working to reintroduce it. This means we have sheep to thank for the invention of shears and scissors. Examples from the Iron Age look remarkably similar to the sheep shears found today: thin, sharp blades connected by a curve or bow of metal.

Wearing Wool

Knitting was predated by nålebinding, which used a needle to sew short lengths of wool together in loops. In London's Victoria & Albert Museum (the V&A), you can find a pair of surprisingly clean-looking socks, excavated from burial grounds in central Egypt. Equally remarkably, they're still bright red in colour, despite being roughly 1,600 years old. Made from three-ply wool using the nålebinding method, they have a split toe, meaning they were designed to be worn with sandals.

True knitting doesn't seem to have appeared until centuries later, perhaps as an evolution of nålebinding. Generally thought to have originated in the Middle East between the sixth and eleventh centuries, it found its way into Spain via Muslim knitters employed by the Royal Palaces – then on into the rest of Europe.

The V&A also holds the earliest scrap of true knitting ever found: part of a blue and cream stocking with an abstract design that echoes the colour combinations and patterning found in Islamic ceramics. Discovered in North Africa, it's dated as 1100–1300 CE, making it more than 900 years old.

Above: Ancient shears, such as this highly decorative pair from the second century CE, bear an uncanny resemblance to modern bow-style hand shears.

Right: All modern sheep can trace their lineages back to the ancient mouflon, which spread out across Europe from central Asia.

A Brief History of Sheep • 9

The Rise and Fall of British Wool

There have always been many different peoples settling in what is now the British Isles. Their presence has had a direct impact on the evolution of sheep and the British wool trade, taking it from one of the world's finest products to an industry in decline.

Origins

Sheep are not indigenous to Britain. First came the ancestors of today's shy, agile, and herding-averse Soay, brought over during the Neolithic period by settlers from northern Europe. These were the domesticated descendants of the wild Mediterranean mouflon and horned sheep of Central Asia. Notably their wool could still be plucked – useful in the days before metal blades.

Some 4,000 years later the Romans founded what became Britain's wool trade and, over time, as England's reputation for fine-quality wool began to grow on the continent of Europe, sheep also grew in importance and numbers. In 50 CE, the Romans established a wool-processing area in Winchester, breeding sheep just for the fleece, not meat, and producing wool so fine it was said to be comparable to a spider's web. This could be because the Romans had brought with them a white, hornless sheep with a long, soft fleece with lustre (shine). Twice the size of the Soay, its fleece was also four times heavier. These sheep evolved into British longwool varieties, including the Cotswold, Wensleydale, and Bluefaced Leicester – all of which still produce exceptional wool. Some of the shortwools also descend from this lineage, including the Ryeland, Oxford, and South Down.

Next came the Danes, who began to arrive around the end of the eighth century CE. Although wool production wasn't seen as being so important during these times, they introduced the blackface, horned sheep, with fleeces ranging from grey to brown. This hardy variety was exceptionally well-suited to the mountains of Scotland and Wales. It had a fleece that produced strong, coarse wool, ideal for making ropes, rugs, and carpets. These sheep developed into the Blackface, Swaledale, and Herdwick breeds of northern Britain.

The Middle Ages saw vast fortunes built on selling wool from curly-coated Cotswold sheep.

A Golden Age

The medieval era saw the beginning of the golden age of wool production, prompting the adage that "half the wealth of England rides on the back of sheep". Between the 13th and 15th centuries, wool made certain members of medieval English society extremely rich, and anyone with land – from peasants to lords – got involved in the trade. Between 1338 and 1339, a wool merchant from Hull, William de la Pole, lent King Edward III around £118,000 (the best part of £167million today). Meanwhile, the Cotswold sheep became known as the Cotswold Lion for its leonine, corkscrew curls – fleeces that paid for most of the area's famed golden buildings. The finest wool (likened to silk) was said to come from Leominster in Herefordshire, from the Lemstore Ore (now the Ryeland). Apparently Queen Elizabeth I so loved her gift of woollen stockings made from this wool, she declared she'd henceforth wear clothing made from nothing else.

Probable Lines of Evolution of British Sheep Breeds

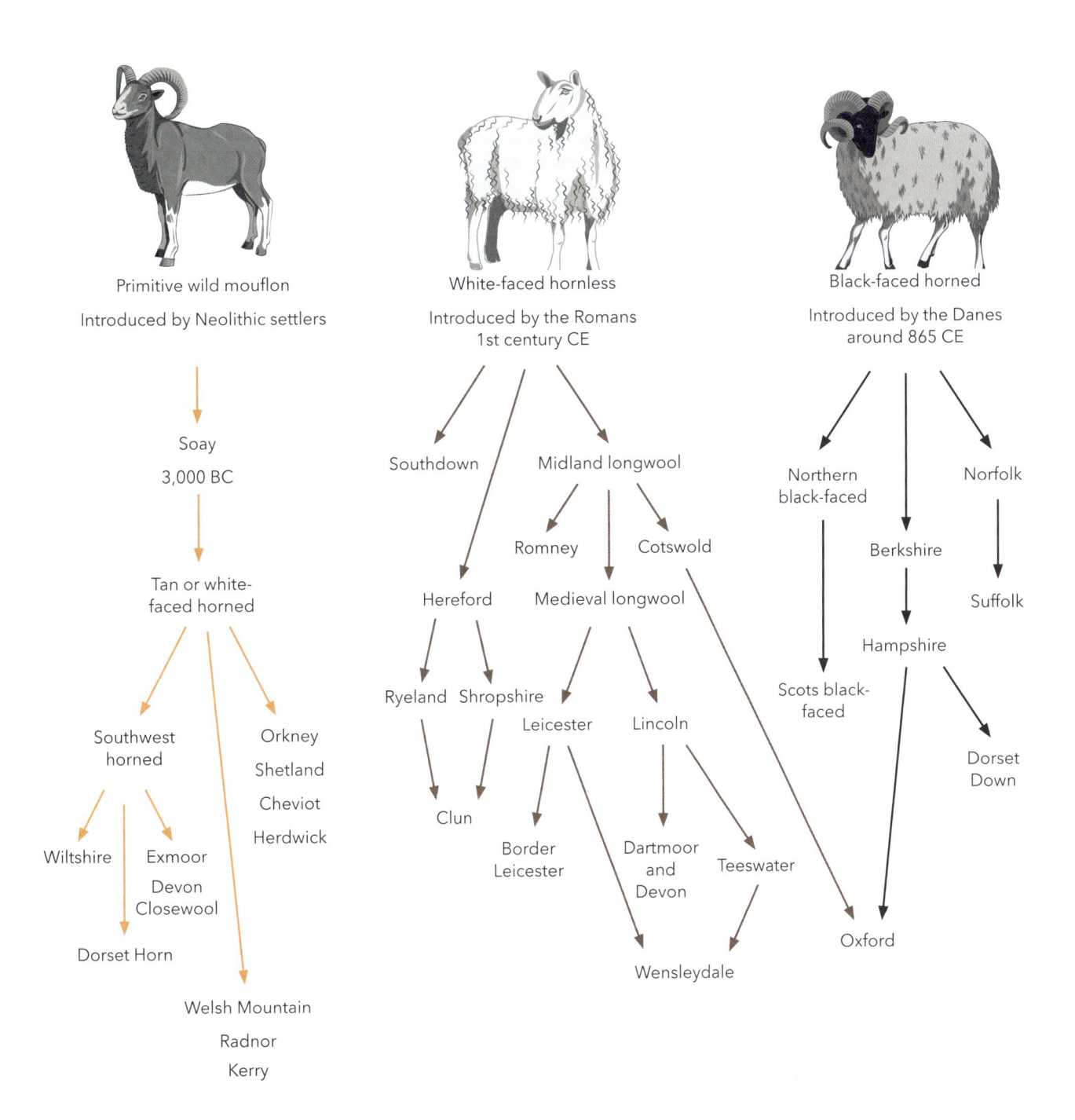

Primitive wild mouflon
Introduced by Neolithic settlers

- Soay 3,000 BC
- Tan or white-faced horned
  - Southwest horned
    - Wiltshire
    - Exmoor
    - Devon Closewool
    - Dorset Horn
  - Orkney
  - Shetland
  - Cheviot
  - Herdwick
  - Welsh Mountain
  - Radnor
  - Kerry

White-faced hornless
Introduced by the Romans 1st century CE

- Southdown
- Midland longwool
  - Romney
  - Cotswold
  - Hereford
    - Ryeland
    - Shropshire
      - Clun
  - Medieval longwool
    - Leicester
      - Border Leicester
    - Lincoln
      - Dartmoor and Devon
      - Teeswater
    - Wensleydale

Black-faced horned
Introduced by the Danes around 865 CE

- Northern black-faced
  - Scots black-faced
- Berkshire
  - Hampshire
    - Dorset Down
    - Oxford
- Norfolk
  - Suffolk

This table is based on the extensive research of Ryder, Michael L., Principal Scientific Officer, Animal Breeding Research Organisation (ABRO), Edinburgh. 'The history of sheep breeds in Britain', Agricultural History Review, 12 (1964), 1-12, 65-82.

Thriving Flocks

For once, Britain's rainy climate gave it the edge when it came to sheep: the wet weather ensuring a longer grazing season and plenty of lush grass on which the sheep could thrive. 'Thriving' is an adjective that could also be applied to their owners. Between 1317 and 1321, a sack of Ryeland wool weighing 165kg (364lb) would have been worth an enormous sum of money – the equivalent of around £3,000 today. As the Ryeland has since been crossed numerous times – producing more meat and a lower quality fleece – an equivalent bag of wool would now only fetch around £180. Yet since the 14th century, the Lord Speaker in the British House of Lords has sat on the "Woolsack" to reflect the economic importance of the wool trade in England. Resembling a large square cushion covered in red cloth, the Woolsack was restuffed in 1938 with a blend of wool from Britain and the other wool-producing nations of the Commonwealth.

In the Middle Ages, large monastic estates were particularly successful wool producers. By 1322, Canterbury Priory was running 14,000 sheep on 40 manors, with an average flock size of about 340. The Cistercian monks, who'd migrated from France the previous century, were the most successful of the monastic wool producers. Most of their 50 monasteries had agricultural estates with the specific purpose of breeding sheep for wool export. Fifteen of these were in Yorkshire, where by 1315 their sheep totalled 250,000. Adhering to the rigidly centralist system within the order, the monks produced a superior product, preparing their clip carefully as demanded by the Florentine merchants. Ensuring it was free of clack, lok, cot and breech (marked, daggy, tangled wool, including from the haunches) meant they achieved more for their efforts than most other producers.

Ports such as London, Southampton, Boston, and Hull expanded to cope with the ever-increasing volume of exports. Many farmers, middlemen, and landowners involved in the trade went on to build some of England's finest houses and prettiest villages, including Chipping Camden, Stow-on-the-Wold, and Bury St Edmunds. Lavenham, in Suffolk, with its fine timber-framed buildings and beautiful church, is said to be the best example of a medieval wool town. At the time it was the fourteenth wealthiest in England, despite its relative compactness. Norwich, as a key point of connection within the wool trade, enjoyed second-city status.

With fleeces being sold into Italy, a sophisticated trade in forward-options on future clips had begun. Wool traders (mostly Italian merchants) would agree to buy three or four years' worth of wool in advance, sometimes betting on a wool clip as much as 20 years before the sheep were actually shorn. These merchants charged high interest on what were essentially loans, typically between 10 and 40 per cent. One family, the infamous Medicis, was so good at trading they went from small-scale wool traders to global bankers and a political dynasty in just a few generations.

Changes in Land and Diet

In order to take in enough nutrition, a sheep will graze for eight to ten hours a day and needs large tracts of land to do so. By 1500 there were three sheep to every person in England. With wool being so profitable, a process began of enclosing previously open fields to keep animals confined and make farming more efficient. Across Britain, vast swathes of open land were fenced off, and sheep were brought in from the bare fallows, heaths, and downs. Both the enclosures and the Dissolution of the Monasteries (from 1536) caused huge suffering in the rural population. The people's subsistence way of living was destroyed as they lost access to much of the land they had previously worked, and many of those displaced migrated to towns and cities in search of factory work, meaning an increased demand for meat.

Often, a sheep's natural diet of grass was replaced with clover and turnips. This enabled farmers to meet the need for more meat, but the turnips were often too hard for a sheep's teeth, causing them to erode more quickly. This shortened the animal's natural lifespan of roughly seven years. The richer diet also damaged the quality of the wool, making it coarser. Wool was still big business, but the growth of the cotton industry was beginning to challenge its dominance. Cotton was cheaper, more versatile, easier to process, and created lighter and, at the time, more comfortable garments.

The aptly named Ram Inn once dominated Minchinhampton's market square, overlooking honey-coloured houses and Holy Trinity Church.

Opposite page: Washed sheep fleece, air-drying on racks before being spun into yarn.

The Rise and Fall of British Wool · 13

A Slow Decline

By the 16th century the British wool trade was at the start of its slow decline. Many traders were beginning to switch to Spanish merino (developed by a tribe of Arabic Moors in the 12th century). There were some attempts to turn the tide. For instance, in 1571 a law was passed stating that all Englishmen, except for nobles, had to wear a woollen cap to church on Sundays. Then, in 1614, James I issued a proclamation banning the export of wool. This was repeated in 1617 and enshrined in law in 1660. As part of a broader strategy of mercantilism, the ban was designed to increase the export of finished goods, rather than raw materials, while also aiming to halt the growth of the Flemish textile industries. Ironically, many Flemish weavers had migrated to England in the previous two centuries, their skills kickstarting Britain's textile industry.

Occasionally, particularly draconian measures were introduced to enforce the ban. In the coastal regions of Kent and Sussex the smuggling of wool to France was rife because of the high prices it could fetch. A 1698 Act of Parliament decreed that sheep-keepers living within ten miles of the coast "shall be obliged to give an exact account, within three days of shearing" of the number and weight of their fleeces and what they'd done with them.

As more and more people migrated to work in the cities, landowners took the opportunity to enclose more and more land. In the 18th century, enclosures caused even greater devastation in the Scottish Highlands, when tens of thousands of Highlanders were thrown off their traditional holdings to make way for more profitable livestock. A century later there would be little unenclosed land left in Britain, and what remained was largely rough mountain pasture, forest, and village greens. Today the legacy of the land enclosures lives on. Half of England is owned by just 25,000 landowners – less than 1 per cent of its population.

For a while, the new Highland sheep farms were a success, and wool prices almost doubled between the 1850s and 1860s. However, at the end of the 19th century, the Highland sheep industry was decimated by a toxic mix of greed, bad luck, and foreign competition. Many sheep estates were overstocked, and the land simply couldn't cope. With not enough grass to eat, the sheep failed to thrive, declined in quality, and became much more susceptible to disease.

The Industrial Revolution also had a significant impact. While wool production benefited from mechanization, the cotton industry surged ahead, reducing wool's importance in the overall textile market. Meanwhile, with more and more people living in cities, selective breeding of sheep started focusing on dual-purpose breeds that were good for both wool and meat. Over time, meat became the more valuable element, partly because of improvements in transportation (railways and refrigeration).

In the coastal regions of Kent and Sussex the smuggling of wool to France was rife because of the high prices it could fetch

The Rise of Synthetic Fibres

By the 1960s and 1970s, meat production had become more economically important than wool for many sheep farmers, particularly as they faced competition from synthetic fibres and cheaper wool from America, Australia, and New Zealand. These countries embraced large-scale agricultural production, enabling them to aggressively undercut British prices. This meant that by the mid-1980s, 70 per cent of the wool being used in Britain came from overseas.

In 2019, the educator and writer Clara Parkes – author of the book *Vanishing Fleece* – gave an impassioned talk about the need to protect the wool industry (you can watch the talk on YouTube). She begins with the statistic that in 1949, 76 per cent of sweaters worn by Americans were made from wool. Ten years later, the figure was just 17 per cent, and today only 1 per cent of the clothes worn globally are woollen. Parkes adds that in the 1960s, 10 per cent of Americans' household income was spent on clothing and shoes – which would buy you about 25 items. Today, the spend is just 3 per cent, but it now buys around 75 items. And consider that a staggering 69 per cent of global fibre production is from synthetic, oil-based materials – which remain in landfill for generations.

Parkes talks about the PR war waged by the producers of synthetic fibres, which became popular in the years after World War II (when factories needed to switch from making ammunitions to something new). Slogans like "Sheep wish they could be this soft and cosy" helped embed in popular culture the idea that wool is heavy, hard to wash, and itchy. Today's technology has negated all of these issues. Wool can be gossamer-light, easy to wash (even in the machine), and non-itchy.

Meanwhile, synthetic fibres have proven to be both highly flammable and capable of releasing thousands of microplastics and nanoplastics into water during the washing process. These plastic fragments are now found on every part of the planet: buried in Arctic sea ice; inside the guts of marine animals who inhabit the deepest ocean trenches; in the soil; even in beer and honey. A 2024 study by researchers at Columbia and Rutgers Universities in the US found that the average litre of bottled water contains some 240,000 detectable plastic fragments – 10 to 100 times greater than previous estimates. These minute particles can pass into human blood, cells, and through the placenta to unborn foetuses, with unknown health effects for everyone.

Campaigning for Wool

Over the decades, and in order to counteract the negative messages about wool, different countries have run extremely successful PR campaigns, including today's global Campaign for Wool. Established in the UK in 2010 by King Charles III, who is still its patron, the campaign partners with key nations, including Australia, South Africa, New Zealand, Korea, Japan, and China, along with many countries in Europe. The @campaignforwool Instagram account has many inspiring posts.

Today's sheep are still cross-bred primarily for their meat, while British knitwear companies buy their wool from abroad at half the price they'd pay locally. And although in recent years the wool market has begun to show steady global growth (from $10 billion in 2023 to $10.79 billion in 2024), there is still much to be done to promote it on a worldwide scale.

Harlequin cardigan, created with the wool of 11 rare sheep breeds, showcasing the variety of natural colours available. A design collaboration with Miriam Greaves and Ossian knitwear.

The Wonder of Wool

It's hard to set a sheep on fire, not that you'd want to try... This is because, despite the fact that wool can be soft as silk, its fleece is also tough enough to resist flames. A high nitrogen and water content mean that it only lights at around 570-600°C, then just tends to smoulder and char.

This is one example of the versatility of a fibre that has been woven, knitted, and felted into the centre of our culture. Another is that it can keep you warm as toast or cool as a cucumber. A third is that it's fantastically robust. Resistant to tearing and abrasion, it's naturally elastic and capable of stretching then returning to its original shape.

Wool is not hair, but a fibre with a hidden structure. This includes natural barbs, or scales, which can attach to one another. These scales (arranged like slates on a roof) repel water. But water vapour can slip between the small cracks, where it's absorbed and held inside the core of the fibre. This is what makes wool easy to dye.

As it's also a brilliant insulator, wool is highly effective when used to line the cavities in the walls of buildings – a fact that we don't exploit nearly enough. Air trapped between the fibres creates a thermal barrier. For as fleece absorbs moisture it gives off heat, meaning that large piles of wool can become hot all by themselves.

And, if all that's not enough, wool is UV-protective, anti-bacterial, self-cleaning, odour resistant, hypoallergenic, and 100 per cent biodegradable.

In addition to the wool itself, sheep also produce lanolin. Made by the sebaceous glands in the sheep's skin, lanolin coats the wool fibres, giving both the skin and fleece an extra layer of protection against the elements – a kind of sheep's sunscreen. It's used in cosmetics and for softening our skin. It's also the perfect protection for nipples when breastfeeding, and has a light antiseptic quality. Another use is in helping to prevent rust, making it a popular product in boat building and engineering.

Wool forms part of the natural carbon cycle. Sheep consume organic carbon by eating plants and store this in their fleece. This means that 50 per cent of a fleece's weight is pure organic carbon, stored in a durable, wearable form. When used in interior textiles such as carpets and upholstery, wool absorbs and locks away pollutants such as volatile organic carbons (VOCs) from the air more rapidly than other fibres.

Right: The design of modern moccasins worn by sheep shearers has changed little since the Middle Ages.

Opposite page: Romney/Shetland crosses in full fleece, waiting for the shearer.

Sheep Shearing

With the exception of a few breeds, sheep don't self-moult, so annual shearing is essential for their welfare. Left unsheared, sheep are susceptible to insect infestations (such as blowfly strike) and heat exhaustion. They'll also develop itches and start rubbing, which can lead to injuries. Electric clippers offer speed and efficiency, while hand shears are quieter, so possibly less stressful. Hand shearing also leaves a short layer of wool, giving the sheep some protection from the weather. Although whichever way the fleece is removed, unless conditions are very cold it only takes the sheep a matter of hours to acclimatise.

If you don't clip a sheep, its wool will just keep growing. Over the years, stories have emerged illustrating how extreme unshorn fleeces can become. Shrek the merino sheep became a hero in New Zealand when he was found with a fleece that weighed 27kg (60lb), having lived alone in a cave for six years. An Australian merino, Chris, who'd also been living wild, was recaptured with a fleece weighing a staggering 40kg (88lb).

Shearing is a job that calls for strength, skill and stamina. Whether using hand shears or electric clippers, professional shearers aim to get the fleece off every sheep as efficiently and cleanly as possible, with minimal stress and no cuts. Although many professionals can shear a sheep in under a minute, commercial shearing isn't necessarily about speed. Competitions, on the other hand, are. In 2024 a Scottish woman, Una Cameron achieved a world record, aged 51, shearing 517 sheep over a nine-hour period with just four breaks. Her mammoth effort was said to be the equivalent of running two marathons back-to-back.

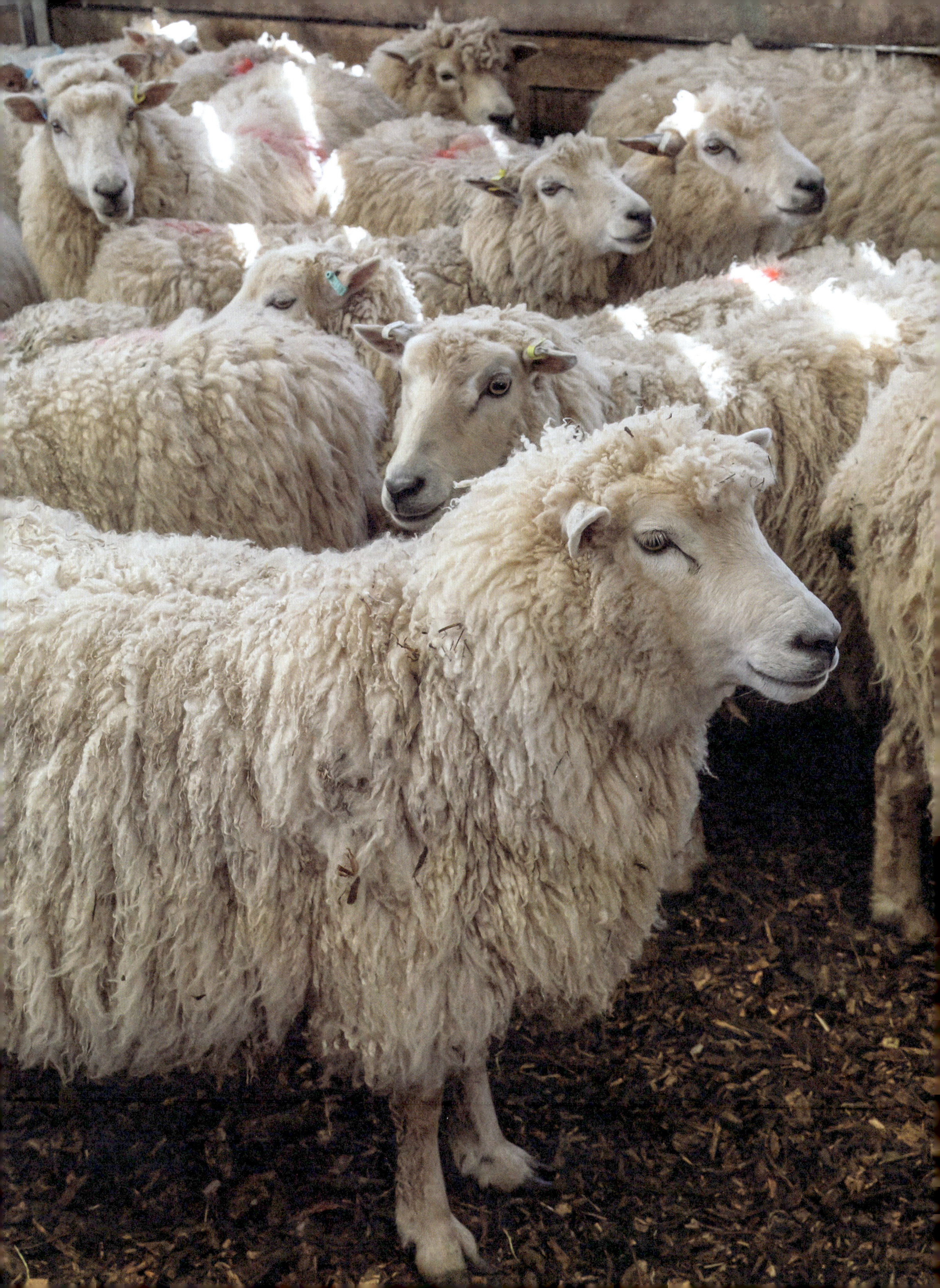

Choosing a New Direction

When it comes to wool and the clothes we make from it, we need to consider sustainable solutions that don't involve animal suffering or environmental damage. We also need to consider the importance of breed diversity.

Britain has a greater variety of sheep than any other country, possibly due to its varying terrain. And each breed has adapted to its unique environment: Romneys thrive in damp marshes, while Blackface mountain sheep survive on thistles and lower-grade grasses. With our climate changing, we don't know which specific characteristics will be needed in the future, so it's essential we ensure that these breeds, and their genetic diversity, are protected. However, many rare breeds are in danger of extinction – mostly due to sheep having been prioritized for their meat, and the fact that breeds are dying out with their breeders. Every year the Rare Breeds Survival Trust issues a list of those that are endangered, to try and prevent them from disappearing.

In terms of animal welfare, over the last few years PETA (People for Ethical Treatment of Animals) has exposed the terrible treatment of rabbits in the production of angora yarn, goats in the production of mohair and cashmere, and sheep in the production of Australian merino wool.

All of these point to the fact that we need some new ways of thinking.

Organic and Regenerative Farming

For the last 60 years, farming has been heavily reliant on large-scale, intensive systems, which have had a drastically detrimental effect on the land. In 2014 the UN warned that soils around the world are heading for exhaustion and depletion, with only an estimated 60 harvests left. At the same time, British farmers were advised that the UK is just 30 to 40 years away from the fundamental eradication of soil fertility if we continue to farm so intensively. Organic and regenerative farming both offer possible solutions; these involve using non-intensive methods that can still achieve excellent results.

Organic farming is built on four key principles: health, ecology, care, and fairness. In practice this means that as a last resort farmers can use a very limited number of naturally derived pesticides, but no routine antibiotics or artificial fertilizers. They must rest the land and support local biodiversities, relying on manure and nitrogen-rich plants like clover instead of genetically modified feed. They must also achieve the highest welfare standards for their animals through focusing on good animal husbandry.

Such stringent regulations have meant some farmers have found the system too complicated and expensive to work for them. A growing alternative is regenerative (or agroecological) farming. This approach is rooted in indigenous practices, working in harmony with the land to maintain and restore natural ecosystems, including regenerating the soil. Unlike organic farming, there are no strict regulations that must be followed; it's more about farming as we once knew it.

Sheep farming within this system often means moving the sheep to fresh pasture every one to three days, mimicking the natural movement of a flock through the landscape. This return to grass feeding is beneficial for the sheep's teeth and fleece. It also reduces the need for chemical fertilizers, instead using the natural fertilizing properties of the sheep's dung – which improves the quality of the soil. Resting the land for long periods enables the grass to grow deep roots, creating a sponge-like soil that holds water and helps to mitigate against flood and drought. The roots (like wool itself) also sequester carbon (they capture and store atmospheric carbon dioxide), which again helps the planet.

These kinds of practices work particularly well on small-scale farms, where the costs of feed and fertilizer can be crippling. One way in which these farmers are working to secure their future is through diversifying their activities. This includes working more directly with the general public, for instance by selling their produce at farmers' markets. The Rare Breeds Survival Trust has encouraged many of these smallholders to take on rare breed sheep, partly because of the distinctive flavours of their meat. Fortuitously, the farmers' holistic practices are also seeing them produce exceptional quality wool.

Britain has a greater variety of sheep than any other country, possibly due to its varying terrain

Stop Fast Fashion

Slow fashion is the perfect antidote to fast. It supports quality – as opposed to fleeting trends – encouraging people to invest in well-made, longer-lasting clothes.

In 2010, the Fibershed movement was started in California by weaver and natural dyer Rebecca Burgess, with the aim of promoting "local fibres, local dyes, and local labour". Today it's an international community, consisting of scores of regional networks of farmers, processors, designers, makers, and consumers. One of the Fibershed approaches to fashion is for designers and makers to become an integral part of the fibre supply network. So a designer, rather than simply choosing wools and swatches from a visiting agent, might instead find a farmer or a flock, then find spinners and dyers, knitters and processors, all within their local network.

Another idea is that the fashion industry could follow the farming year, perhaps only presenting new collections around autumn harvest time. This slower approach would give more time for communication, research, and partnership building.

While Fibershed aims to operate on a sustainable but commercial scale, albeit it in regional networks, perhaps the best example of slow fashion is a garment you've made yourself. Fashion writer Jonathan Chapman coined the term "emotional durability" to describe the effect of producing a garment you'll treasure for a lifetime, reducing the need to buy excessively.

Between 2000 and 2014, the number of garments produced doubled to 100 billion annually – or as McKinsey researchers noted, fourteen new garments per person per year for every person on the planet. If we all scaled back our purchasing habits to match what we bought fifty years ago, we could cut carbon emissions by 1.2 per cent. Learning new skills, such as fleece processing, spinning, and knitting, are all positive contributions towards achieving this.

British rare breeds can be used to help regenerate the wool industry in the UK and internationally. It's possible to create sustainable yarns that provide 100 per cent biodegradable, natural alternatives to the synthetic products that currently dominate the market. A yarn that can perform as well as synthetic fleece must be light, soft to touch, and priced fairly for the farmer (and end consumer). With innovative practices, plus careful selective breeding, this is entirely achievable. We can also produce wools with different yarn effects – including lofty (hairy) ones like mohair – to replace angora and alpaca, while giving an equally pleasurable knitting experience.

Another possibility would be to extend the range of fibres we produce, for instance mixing wool with linen – maybe growing our own flax (this is already happening on a small scale and showing excellent growth potential). Instead, in the UK we continue to primarily focus on importing fibres from other parts of the world, many with questionable issues when it comes to animal welfare. Again, this is an area where we're already ahead of the game, our welfare standards being some of the strictest and most comprehensive. And it's well within our ability to produce versions of yarns like cashmere and merino, thus reducing their carbon footprint.

Combine this with organic and regenerative farming – and a bit of innovation, investment, and imagination – and Britain could easily become a leader in the production of one of the world's most ethical, quality fibres. Imagine that: British wool, in all its new varieties, once more revered internationally.

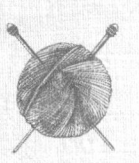

BREED DIRECTORY

Black Welsh Mountain	Hebridean	Balwen	Jacob
Blue Faced Leicester	Cheviot	Masham	Castlemilk Moorit
Soay	Manx Loaghtan	Leicester Longwool	Ryeland
British Milk Sheep	Wensleydale	Romney	Boreray
South Downs	Teeswater	Portland	Oxford Down

Categorization: Old and New

Historically, British sheep originated from three main sources: longwools and a few shortwools from the Romans; mountain breeds from the Vikings; and Soay from the primitives. These latter sheep existed before people started farming. After centuries of selective breeding, Australia and New Zealand now produce the finest wool in the world, courtesy of their merinos. However, what Britain lacks in terms of softness is made up for with the diversity of colours and textures that can be found in its 60-plus pure breeds. This variety is greater than in any other country, forming a natural resource that (properly exploited) can offer an equally unique range of knitted items.

The term "pure breed" is slightly misleading, for over the centuries most sheep have been cross-bred. However, British Wool's *Guide to British Sheep Breeds* categorizes them in this way, so this book follows the same method. Each breed is well adapted to local environments, landscapes, and farming practices. This makes them integral to Britain's agricultural heritage, valued not only for their wool but also their role in maintaining the biodiversity and landscapes of the regions where they originated (or have migrated to and thrived).

Britain's Ancient Breeds

Having knitted the wool of all 62 breeds, I became aware of the huge diversity of hand feels, colours, and textures. For simplicity, the Breed Directory over the following pages is divided into three categories: primitives, longwools, and downs and shortwools. These are based solely on fleece types (not heritage). Of the 30 breeds the directory highlights, all have been chosen for their suitability for hand-knitting. Some of the fleece produced by these breeds does have a coarser handle (hand feel), but they have been included due to their unique colour, or the fact that they produce a soft undercoat. If meticulously sorted, this can produce a fine yarn. The ten knitting projects use the wool from the 12 sheep that I found in my research to be the softest.

Although the Shetland sheep produces one of the finest fleeces, it's already known worldwide so is not included here, for this is a book that highlights the lesser-known breeds. As interest in native breeds grows and farmers see a financial benefit from selling their fleece for wool, they'll be encouraged to selectively breed sheep for fleece quality – as in the Middle Ages when Britain produced some of the world's finest wool. It won't take many generations of breeding to once again improve fleece quality dramatically, and farmers who are ahead of the game are already seeing results.

Counting Sheep

There are no population figures included in the Breed Directory. This is because they're almost impossible to find. Many of the breed societies don't have every flock registered with them, and figures change all the time. Where possible, information is given on whether a sheep breed is endangered (meaning there are less than 1,000 that are known), or at-risk (meaning there are 1,000–5,000 recorded within the UK).

For each breed, you'll find a brief description, plus wool characteristics and tips for spinners and knitters.

Woollen or Worsted Spun?

According to the fleece's staple, it needs to be worsted spun or woollen spun in order to produce the wool (yarn). This can vary between sheep in each of the three categories.

Woollen spun is when a fleece with a shorter staple is carded with brushes. This produces a more matt and lofty yarn.

Worsted spun is when combs are used on longer staple lengths. This produces a much smoother, durable (and sometimes soft) yarn.

Woolly Words

Crimp: the level of coil and waviness in strands of wool

Handle: how soft or coarse a fleece or yarn feels in your hand

Kemp: short white hairs, often found in outer coats, that feel wiry, brittle, and itchy

Loft: the airiness, hairiness, and fluffiness of spun yarn

Lustre: the shine and gloss on raw fleece or spun yarn

Staple: the length of an individual strand of wool from root to tip

The Primitive Breeds

Of the three categories, the primitives are the cleverest sheep, not having been bred for docile domesticity. Consequently, farmers have found them almost impossible to herd – but still love them anyway! Naturally thriving in the remotest areas, these breeds have always used their initiative to survive the hardest, highest, and wettest conditions. Their inaccessible locations meant they avoided the so-called "improvements" of the 18th century (selective breeding for meat) and as a result they have kept their fine, diverse quality of fleece. Some sheep within this category still self-moult – meaning the wool can be hard to collect. The primitives produce a soft, colourful range of shorter wool staples. This category includes a few of the mountain breeds from the Viking lineage that have kept their soft undercoat. Some sheep (including the Boreray and North Ronaldsay) have an underlayer that, separated out, makes an exceptionally soft yarn. Due to the shorter staple, these fleece types are usually woollen spun and can also be blended with longwool fleece to produce a more durable yarn, suitable for a wide range of knitting and weaving projects.

The Longwool Breeds

The finest wool descends from Roman lineage, and the longwools are descended from the Roman white sheep. Breeds like the Teeswater and Leicester Longwool thrive in areas such as Leicestershire and Yorkshire, while the Romneys do well in the southeast, where they've adapted to the damp conditions. Personality-wise, longwools are generally known as being gentle and placid – mostly because they have no desire to escape captivity (they often can't see very well because of the fleece obstructing their eyes). Longwool fleece has a staple that can reach 30cm (12in). It protects the sheep from inclement weather and means they produce the most wool of the three categories. The fleece has a natural twist and sheen, making a soft, shiny, and durable yarn that has a unique lustre and is reluctant to felt. Due to its staple length, the fleece needs to be combed (not carded), which produces a worsted yarn that's perfect for weaving and knitting.

The Down and Shortwool Breeds

Some of the downland breeds are also descended from the Romans, but have a very different wool type: shorter, more compact, and springy. This may be due to cross-breeding with primitive local sheep. Others still have the lustre of the longwool, but with more of a fuzzy crimp (bounce). Down sheep breeds are often not particularly hardy, preferring meadows and lush grass. Most are found in the middle and south of England as they don't tolerate the sparse vegetation and harsher conditions of the north. This is why, historically, different areas produced different yarns. The Ryeland, for example, once produced the finest wool, but was then bred to become primarily a meat sheep to the detriment of its fleece. The fleece of this group has a short staple with a high crimp and lots of bounce. It needs to be woollen spun, producing a lofty, soft, durable, and versatile yarn that's good for all knitwear, especially cables and textures. It's not the softest to touch, but if only the best bits of the fleece are selected, a much-improved handle is the result.

Categorization: Old and New • 23

The Primitive Breeds

Black Welsh Mountain

Welsh scripts from the Middle Ages refer to black-fleeced mountain sheep. Later, in the mid-19th century, flock masters selected quality black lambs to produce a pure breed. The majority can now be found in mid-Wales and North America.

Small and somewhat timid, these sheep produce true-black fleeces, making them unique among British natives. They are hardy, able to remain outside all year round, and produce a fine-flavoured meat. The rams have attractive horns that curve around their ears.

It's important to support this breed, helping Welsh farmers diversify in an economy where sheep farming is vital.

Wool Characteristics

- The fleece is a dark, springy wool. Non-pure animals are black when young. As they age, the fleece turns browner – the darkest brown of the rare breeds. In pedigree pure breeds, the fleece remains black, developing natural silver highlights as the sheep gets older.
- Staple length: 6-10cm (2½-4in)
- Weight of fleece: 1.25-2kg (2.7-4.4lb)

TIPS FOR SPINNERS AND KNITTERS

- Because it's a native mountain breed, the Black Welsh Mountain has a soft handle.
- The fleece has two layers: a finer undercoat and coarser outercoat, so it needs sorting to achieve the best results.
- The fleece has virtually no kemp. It's lightweight and can be mixed with a white fleece of a similar length to achieve various shades of grey wool suitable for knitting textures and cables.
- The wool is naturally resistant to fading, making it ideal for timeless projects.
- This is a medium-staple fleece so it can be worsted or woollen spun.

Suitable alternatives are the Hebridean, Zwartbles, or black Cheviot.

Boreray

Boreray (once known as Hebridean Black-Faced Boreray) originate from St Kilda, an island west of the Scottish Hebrides. When the human residents evacuated St Kilda in the 1930s, the flocks were too wild to be taken and became a fully feral population that still exists. As a result, these small sheep are difficult to handle.

Their markings can be brown, grey, white, or speckled. Rams have impressive spiralling horns. The breed is thought to have some genetic influences acquired from sheep brought to Scotland during Viking invasions.

The Boreray Sheep Society has been incorporated into the Soay Society as the flocks live on the same group of islands. Flocks are managed to ensure there's the right balance of sheep to grasslands in order to sustain them.

This sheep has the potential to be the closest equivalent to the cashmere goat. However, it's a critical conservation breed, surviving in such small numbers it's in danger of extinction, so more support for its farmers is to be encouraged.

Wool Characteristics

- Fleece colours range from creamy white to tan, grey, and brown. The sheep has a coarser, wirier outercoat and a fine undercoat, which have to be separated or you end up with a very coarse yarn. Both coats shed naturally. Strands have low crimp.
- Staple length: 5-15cm (2-6in)
- Weight of fleece: 1-2kg (2.2-4.4lb)

TIPS FOR SPINNERS AND KNITTERS

- The outer hair coat can be used for weaving. It's very hard-wearing so is suitable for bags or even coats.
- The very fine underhair is perfect for textures, cables, or ribbing and can be worn next to the skin. It's prone to felting so needs to be handled carefully.
- Although the staple can be very long, it's better woollen spun (avoiding the longer kemp-filled outer hair).

Suitable alternatives are the Manx Loaghtan or North Ronaldsay.

The Primitive Breeds

The Primitive Breeds

Castlemilk Moorit

A small, horned, elegant-looking sheep, the Moorit is directly descended from the Soay, having been developed in Scotland on an estate in Castlemilk. It's the result of crossing the Soay, Shetland, Manx Loaghtan, and Wiltshire Horn.

The name Moorit means "reddish-brown" in the old Norse language of Orkney and reflects the breed's fleece colour. A smattering of white markings on the jaw come courtesy of Soay genetics.

These sheep are self-reliant (meaning they don't usually need help with lambing) and they're resistant to many common diseases. Unlike other primitive breeds, they have no desire to escape for adventure and will graze contentedly.

Although it's at-risk, the Castlemilk Moorit is growing in popularity.

Wool Characteristics

- The fleece is very soft, fluffy, and brown. The strands get sun-bleached towards the tips, which gives the wool the effect of multicoloured tones.
- Staple length: 4–12cm (1½–4¾in)
- Weight of fleece: 1–1.5kg (2.2–3.3lb)

TIPS FOR SPINNERS AND KNITTERS

- The reddish-brown tone is unique to the breed and blends well with other fibres, specifically alpaca.
- Works well in knitting projects such as Aran jumpers as it gives a soft but defined look.
- This rare wool is generally only processed by farmers so beware its oily handle – which does wash out successfully.
- This is often a short-staple fleece so should be woollen spun.

Suitable alternatives are the Manx Loaghtan or Soay.

26 · Castlemilk Moorit

Hebridean

This is a small sheep, mostly black, although it may become grey with age. Both males and females have two or four large horns and slender legs. The breed was developed in the ninth century on the Hebridean islands off the west coast of Scotland. Quite wild in nature, Hebridean sheep remain resolutely primitive.

Perfectly suited to damp climates and coastal weather, these sheep have a double coat. The undercoat is warm and insulating, while the top coat is coarser and water-resistant.

The breed is found throughout the UK and is increasingly popular with smallholders. It's widely used in conservation grazing schemes.

Wool Characteristics

- The fleece produces exceptionally dark wool, almost black, with dark brown and grey flecks.
- Staple length: 5-15cm (2-6in)
- Weight of fleece: 1.25-2.25kg (2.7-5lb)

TIPS FOR SPINNERS AND KNITTERS

- Hebridean wool is becoming increasingly popular due to its soft handle. It's often blended with other breeds to create shades of grey. Pure and blended types can be purchased from some of the big spinning mills.
- As well as being soft, the yarn is durable. Wool from the top coat is prone to containing kemp, which needs to be removed otherwise it can be itchy.
- Being a naturally dark colour that doesn't fade, it's great for designs needing a strong contrast colour , such as Fair Isle or intarsia.
- It has a medium staple length so can be worsted or woollen spun.

A suitable alternative is the Black Welsh Mountain.

The Primitive Breeds

The Primitive Breeds

Herdwick

Regarded as the hardiest of the British breeds, the Herdwick is able to survive on the highest grounds. It has a white head and legs. It's the friendliest sheep, making a great pet, and loves having its face scratched.

Recorded in 12th-century documents, it's believed to have originated in Scandinavia but was developed across the centuries on the Lake District fells. The name was originally spelt Herdwyck and means "sheep pasture".

In the later years of her life, the children's author Beatrix Potter kept and bred Herdwicks, acting as the Herdwick Society's president for a time, and winning various prizes across Cumbria. On her death she bequeathed 1,600 hectares (4,000 acres) to the National Trust in order to continue the grazing of Herdwick flocks.

Wool Characteristics

- The fleece is grey; lambs are born black and become grey as they mature.
- Staple length: 10-20cm (4-8in)
- Weight of fleece: 1.5-2kg (3.3-4.4lb)

TIPS FOR SPINNERS AND KNITTERS

- The fleece is coarse, so not suitable for general knitting.
- It works well for knitted slippers, outerwear, and woven rugs due to its durability. The Herdwick is a popular breed and the wool is commercially available.
- Its short staple means it tends to be woollen spun.

Suitable alternatives are the Boreray or Jacob.

28 • Herdwick

Jacob

Jacob sheep have unique multicoloured coats and striking black-and-white faces. Both the male and female have two or four horns, with one set curling down around the ears and the other arching up and back. Lambs are just black and white.

Established in the 17th century, the Jacob is closely related to a Middle Eastern breed from biblical times. Originally kept by the landed gentry as ornamental parkland animals for their picturesque fleece and horns, they are now found across the UK.

The Jacob is one of the most popular of the rare breeds as the animals are attractive, generally good-tempered and easy to manage.

Wool Characteristics

- The fleece naturally has four colours: black, brown, white, and grey. These can be separated or combined to create a wonderful marl yarn. Kemp, if present, can give it the look of tweed. The varied colour palette is a reason for the breed's success. The wool's quality, however, isn't as fine as some other rare breeds.
- Staple length: 8–15cm (3–6in)
- Weight of fleece: 1.5–2.5kg (3.3–5.5lb)

TIPS FOR SPINNERS AND KNITTERS

- Popular with hand spinners as it offers a varied colour palette in a single fleece.
- Its creates versatile, springy yarn that's suitable for pattern and Fair Isle work, textures, and cables. While it's not particularly soft, neither is it itchy, making it suitable for sweaters and accessories.
- The varied length of this fleece makes it suitable for woollen or worsted spinning.

A suitable alternative is the Cheviot.

The Primitive Breeds

The Primitive Breeds

Manx Loaghtan

A small, wiry sheep, the Manx Loaghtan can have two, four, or even six striking horns. The breed developed in the 11th century and is descended from a primitive mountain breed thought to have lived on the Isle of Man for more than 1,000 years. The word "loaghtan" is Manx for mouse-brown. The rams sometimes die when fighting each other because their horns are so heavy they can crack each other's skulls.

It's thought the breed's wool is particularly good because the sheep were isolated on the Isle of Man, so missed out on the cross-breeding that aimed to increase the meat yield.

This is an at-risk breed that needs continued support in order to survive.

Wool Characteristics

- The fleece is a natural nutmeg brown, really soft and silky. It has good springiness but doesn't twist. The springiness comes from a high crimp quality. The yarn has a high lanolin content, meaning it's a great wool for warmth and offers a good amount of natural elasticity.
- Staple length: 6–12cm (2½–4¾in)
- Weight of fleece: 1.5–2kg (3.3–4.4lb)

TIPS FOR SPINNERS AND KNITTERS

- This wool is perfect for textures and Arans. It's also good for knitting socks because it's a lightweight but durable yarn.
- It can have kemp hairs, especially in older sheep. The wool quality can be maintained with careful sorting.
- Varying staple lengths within the fleece allow it to be worsted or woollen spun, producing a smooth or lofty yarn accordingly. Both are highly versatile.

A suitable alternative is the Castlemilk Moorit.

30 · Manx Loaghtan

North Ronaldsay

Tenacious, hardy, highly adaptable, and prolific, North Ronaldsay sheep are used to living in the rocks around the island after which they are named. They're small, fine boned, and have furry faces. The rams are horned.

This ancient breed of northern European sheep predates the Iron Age. It came originally from the islands of Orkney and has learned to survive entirely on seaweed, which results in an exceptionally soft fleece. It's one of the few animals to have adapted in this way, and now it can't eat grass. This means it will always be a rare breed unless it's possible to change its diet.

Due to it's very specific adaptations, this is an endangered breed.

Wool Characteristics

- The exceptionally soft fleece comes in white, greys, browns, and beiges.
- Staple length: 4–10cm (1½–4in)
- Weight of fleece: 1.5–2.5kg (3.3–5.5lb)

TIPS FOR SPINNERS AND KNITTERS

- The fleece has a soft undercoat. If carefully separated from the outercoat it can produce an exceptionally soft yarn.
- The fibre tends to matt at the base of each strand, so felts easily. It can be difficult to card the wool unless you untangle it first.
- The soft undercoat can be spun into a fine lightweight yarn. This is great for knitting delicate lace shawls or next-to-the-skin garments.
- A medium staple means it can be worsted or woollen spun (carefully!).

Suitable alternatives are the Hebridean or Boreray.

The Primitive Breeds

The Primitive Breeds

Portland

The prettiest of sheep, the Portland is small and stoic with a tan face and light-coloured horns. As the rams age, their horns spiral outwards.

This is an ancient breed, once common in Dorset in the south of England. It originated on the Isle of Portland, which is possibly the reason it escaped the meat "improvement" efforts of the 18th century.

It's said to be very independent and not easily intimidated – a sheep with a sense of its own dignity. These are also tough animals, able to live outside all year in harsh weather and flourish on most terrains.

Owing to their small size and ability to thrive on low-quality grasses, Portlands are able to be kept at a higher density per acre than many other sheep. They are capable of lambing out of season, generally producing single offspring and needing minimal intervention.

Wool Characteristics

- The fleece is a foxy red when the lambs are born, turning to a white or soft grey in adulthood. However, the sheep never lose the gingery/tannish hue on their faces and legs. With careful selection this breed can produce an exceptionally versatile wool.
- Staple length: 5–9cm (2–3½in)
- Weight of fleece: 1.5–2.5kg (3.3–5.5lb)

TIPS FOR SPINNERS AND KNITTERS

- The fleece varies from sheep to sheep, ranging from a really soft handle to being slightly rugged when knitted.
- It has a lovely honey hue – a soft caramel white that's quite unique. This has made the breed a favourite with stately homes (for the ornamental look of the sheep) and the fleece popular with hand spinners and crafters.
- Its distinctive colour, and soft, lightweight handle makes it ideal for luxury items such as shawls and statement cable knit sweaters.
- Its short staple means it needs to be woollen spun.

A suitable alternative is the Cheviot.

Soay

Soay sheep are the most primitive of the British native breeds and originate from the St Kilda archipelago off Scotland's west coast. This is an extremely rare breed, genetically closest to the original Mouflon of northern Europe. When they run semi-wild they're difficult to control – they very much have their own minds and need minimum human intervention in order to survive.

These are small sheep, with horns and no wool on their face or legs. As the breed developed in harsh island conditions, these are excellent, hardy foragers. They're also highly resistant to disease, and naturally shed their fleeces.

Wool Characteristics

- Soay fleece is fine and short, generally brown in colour – merging from dark brown at the base to a pale tan at the tip of each strand. As is typical of the primitive breeds, it has two coats. The undercoat is finer and softer, so choose this section if sorting your own fleece. This is still a very rare yarn to find – and will vary from spinner to spinner so be aware of possible differences in tension (gauge) swatches.
- Staple length: 4–10cm (1½–4in)
- Weight of fleece: 350g–1kg (¾–2.2lb)

TIPS FOR SPINNERS AND KNITTERS

- The colour is beautiful and lovely to use in Fair Isles – particularly in combination with white.
- The wool gives a very distinct texture because of the mixture of browns, so this can be used creatively in your pattern work.
- Because the sheep moults naturally you need to card out the skin flakes.
- With a short staple length, it needs to be woollen spun.

Suitable alternatives are the Castlemilk Moorit or Manx Loaghtan.

The Primitive Breeds

Soay · 33

The Longwools

Bluefaced Leicester

The Bluefaced Leicester – or BFL – is one of the UK's bigger breeds. With broad shoulders and a long Roman nose, this is a handsome sheep. Its exceptionally thin face and prominent ears are entirely wool-free.

A direct descendant from the Roman longwool, it evolved in the 18th century in the Tyne and Wear area and Cumbrian hills. It was bred to be crossed with hardy hill sheep to produce high-quality meat and an improved fleece.

Genetically it's weaker than other longwools, and work is being done to make the breed hardier.

Wool Characteristics

- Fleeces range from cream and dark grey to dark brown. The dark brown looks rather like tree bark and is very rare. BFL is the finest and softest wool of all the longwools (close to a cashmere equivalent). For that reason, it's in popular demand. The fleece has spiral locks that are much tighter and not as shiny as other longwools.
- Staple length: 8–15cm (3–6in)
- Weight of fleece: 1–2kg (2.2–4.4lb)

TIPS FOR SPINNERS AND KNITTERS

- This is one of the most predictable fleeces in terms of grade (each fleece is as good as the next). Both the fleece and yarn are expensive to buy, due to their quality and finished softness.
- Bluefaced Leicester is often recommended as a good fleece for beginner spinners as it holds twist easily.
- Easy to knit, and soft on the hands, it's perfect for next-to-the skin sweaters and blended, soft-colour Fair Isles.
- Due to its long staple length, the fleece needs to be worsted spun.

Suitable alternatives are the Romney or Border Leicester.

Border Leicester

This breed is large and hornless, with characteristic long ears and a Roman nose. Its striking appearance and elegant presence mean that it's popular in the show ring. The ears are normally erect – making it look rather like a hare.

Border Leicesters originated in the 18th century through crossing the English Leicester (now extinct) with the Cheviot, a hill breed. As this breed is one of the original longwools, and is a hardy sheep, it could be used in a breeding programme to improve the longevity of the BFL.

In Yorkshire, Doulton Border Leicester Yarn keeps a vegetarian Border Leicester flock – meaning none are slaughtered for meat (see Sourcing Guide).

Wool Characteristics

- This white fleece is soft to handle and semi-lustrous, with moderate sheen or brightness. Each strand of wool has a curl at the tip.
- Staple length: 10-15cm (4-6in)
- Weight of fleece: 3-5kg (6.6-11lb)

TIPS FOR SPINNERS AND KNITTERS

- The white yarn is one of the finest, very clean and soft, making it perfect for textures including Aran and cabling.
- The wool can be fine enough for knitting items like lace shawls.
- Because of its soft handle it's also excellent for knitting babywear.
- Due to its varying staple length, the fleece can be worsted or woollen spun.

Suitable alternatives are the Romney, Bluefaced Leicester, or British Milk Sheep.

The Longwools

The Longwools

British Milk Sheep

This is a robust, hornless sheep of medium size. It has a white face and legs, and a semi-lustrous fleece. It was developed in the 1960s and 1970s by Lawrence Alderson by crossing the Bluefaced Leicester, Dorset, and Lleyn with the Friesland (from Holland) to produce a high-yield dairy ewe. It's a hardy sheep with a gentle temperament.

Many fine cheeses are made from sheep's milk and this breed produces some of the best. It's also known for the quality of its yoghurt. Sadly, though, due to the lack of interest in sheep's cheese in Britain, the breed is highly endangered, with only about 150 remaining – despite the fact that ewes will often produce triplets.

Wool Characteristics

- A creamy white fleece, which creates a soft-handle wool.
- Staple length: 8-14cm (3-5½in)
- Weight of fleece: 2.75-4kg (6-8.8lb)

TIPS FOR SPINNERS AND KNITTERS

- Currently mainly available as fleeces direct from the farmer (see Sourcing Guide), or you can buy the yarn from Ossian Knitwear.
- With careful selection, these fleeces can be turned into one of the best quality yarns, producing things like truly beautiful Aran jumpers.
- A medium staple length means the fleece can either be woollen or worsted spun.

Suitable alternatives are the Romney or Portland.

Cotswold

This is a weighty sheep, first identified as a breed in the 13th century. It's a direct descendant from the sheep imported in the Roman invasion of the first century CE.

The breed's fine wool brought great wealth to the Cotswolds area, which led to prosperous local merchants building grand houses and large churches in stone.

Flocks numbering in the thousands were kept principally for their wool. In medieval times, Gloucester Abbey had over 10,000 sheep.

Cotswold wool provided uniforms for the Roman legions and clothed 18th-century Europe, when made into broadcloth.

Today this is an endangered breed.

Wool Characteristics

- Another of the finest longwools with a natural sheen. The fleece is creamy white with a "golden" quality that visibly shines.
- Staple length: 15-25cm (6-10in)
- Weight of fleece: up to 10kg (22lb)

TIPS FOR SPINNERS AND KNITTERS

- The crimp is very precise – making it particularly rewarding and easy to spin. The curly locks spin into a heavy wool that creates warm and luxurious garments.
- As the yarn is lively and twisty, it tends to roll in on itself. Good for something like moss stitch or gansey, but not so good for Arans.
- With a long staple length, the fleece should be worsted spun.

Suitable alternatives are the Wensleydale or Leicester Longwool.

The Longwools

The Longwools

Greyface Dartmoor

This medium-sized, hornless sheep has a long, thick white fleece along with a furry face, a grey/black mottled nose, and short, woolly legs.

The breed was established in the 17th century, and became famous for its large, heavy fleece, which helps it survive the extremely cold winters on Dartmoor. There is also a Whiteface Dartmoor, which has horns, a thicker fleece, and a white nose. Both varieties have the same thick, curly, lustrous fleece typical of the longwool family.

The ewes make excellent mothers, needing little intervention with birthing.

This breed is currently at risk.

Wool Characteristics

- The heavy fleece is creamy white with open, lustrous curls.
- Staple length: 25-30cm (10-11¾in)
- Weight of fleece: 7-15kg (15.5-33lb)

TIPS FOR SPINNERS AND KNITTERS

- The fleece tends to contain a lot of kemp, but if sorted carefully can produce really nice wool. It's better used for outer garments as it's one of the coarser of the longwools.
- Some of the coarser hairs make great knitted dog leads.
- Due to its long staple length, it needs to be worsted spun.

Suitable alternatives are the Leicester Longwool or Wensleydale.

Leicester Longwool

This is a large, hornless sheep with a charcteristic mop of wool on the crown of its head. It has a white face and legs and fairly long, blue (veiny) ears.

The breed was developed in the 18th century by Robert Bakewell, a major Yorkshire landowner who owned the renowned ram named Bluecap (see Wensleydale). Bakewell selectively bred local Leicester sheep to create a larger, meatier animal, with a long, lustrous, even fleece. His efforts resulted in a sheep that matured earlier and produced more meat and wool. It quickly gained popularity and influenced the development of many other modern breeds.

This is an endangered breed.

Wool Characteristics

- Its wool, and the knitted yarn, is a mixture of cream, light grey, yellow, and creamy brown, giving a wide spectrum of colours within one fleece.
- Staple length: 20-25cm (8-10in)
- Weight of fleece: 5-7kg (11-15.5lb)

TIPS FOR SPINNERS AND KNITTERS

- The yarn was previously perceived as being quite itchy, but a farmer in Wales has, through selective breeding, concentrated on wool quality for more than ten years and now produces an amazingly soft wool. It uniquely combines the sheen common to the longwool family with the loftiness of the Wensleydale and the softness of the Bluefaced Leicester.
- The improved fleece is comparable to mohair – great for knitting plain knits or stripes, or where colours need blending.
- You need to be careful when sourcing your fleece as they can vary from coarse to soft.
- With a long staple length, the fleece should be worsted spun.

Suitable alternatives are the Wensleydale, Teeswater, or Cotswold.

The Longwools

Masham

The Longwools

A hardy sheep without horns, its face and legs are dappled black and white. It has a long, soft, lustrous white fleece. The breed name is pronounced Mas-am – despite the h.

This is a modern hybrid, produced by crossing a Teeswater or Wensleydale ram with a Swaledale or Dalesbred ewe. The result is an animal with the hardy qualities of the hill sheep and the long, lustrous fleece of the longwools. It became a registered breed in 1986.

Mashams are proficient mothers, and the sheep are easy to manage.

Wool Characteristics

- Masham fleece is a natural stone white that can provide a range of colours, from soft white to natural stone and mid-grey when mixed with the fleece of the grey Bluefaced Leicester.
- Staple length: 12-25cm (4¾-10in)
- Weight of fleece: 3-4.5kg (6.6-10lb)

TIPS FOR SPINNERS AND KNITTERS

- The yarn has a beautiful natural lustre.
- The handle is soft and can knit up to make both fine and chunky knitwear that can be worn next to the skin.
- There can be coarser kemp hairs which give the yarn its unique texture and handle.
- By Laxtons offers a Masham and Bluefaced Leicester mix as a commercial yarn (see Sourcing Guide).
- With a long staple length, the fleece should be worsted spun.

Suitable alternatives are the Romney, Border Leicester, or British Milk Sheep.

Romney

The Romney is a hardy and large breed with a friendly, calm nature. It's excellent for both wool and meat. The sheep can be distinguished by a tuft of wool on the forehead, although the modern Romney breeds often don't have this feature.

Developed in the 13th century in the Romney Marsh area of southeast England, the sheep are known locally as Kents. With a direct lineage to the Roman white longwool, it's one of the most ancient breeds and has worldwide popularity in rare breed farming today. The sheep tolerate damp conditions, having adapted to life in marshlands, and the meat is highly rated due to a diet of salt grasses.

A pilot programme is currently underway called "Fabulous Fibre", spearheaded by the UK's National Sheep Association (NSA). If this programme is successful, selective breeding using the Romney will provide a framework for other British pure breeds.

Wool Characteristics

- The large, dense fleece is white or brown. It has a wonderful silky lustre and is one of the softest and easiest to handle. It's classified as semi-lustre longwool.
- Staple length: 15-30cm (6-12in)
- Weight of fleece: 3-7kg (6.6-15.5lb)

TIPS FOR SPINNERS AND KNITTERS

- The fleece has a long, uniform crimp, spins easily, and can be used for most projects.
- The finer parts of the fleece can be used for next-to-skin garments that are machine washable.
- The coarse parts felt well.
- With careful selective breeding, this fleece has the potential to be comparable to the Australian merino.
- As it has a variable staple length, the fleece can be worsted or woollen spun.

Suitable alternatives are the Bluefaced Leicester, Masham, or Border Leicester.

The Longwools

Teeswater

The Teeswater is a large, hornless sheep with a grey and white face. Dark brown markings ring its eyes and nose and it has a woolly forelock that can grow the length of the face.

The breed became well-known in the 19th century, having been bred in Teesdale, County Durham. It's closely related to the Wensleydale and father to the Masham. Like the Wensleydale, it has an exceptionally long, fine, curly fleece. It's bred to produce good meat, as well as quality wool.

Teeswaters are known for their longevity and prolific breeding ability. This is an endangered breed.

Wool Characteristics

- Its long, curly, smooth cream fleece is soft to handle.
- Staple length: 15–30cm (6–11¾in)
- Weight of fleece: 3–6kg (6.6–13.2lb)

TIPS FOR SPINNERS AND KNITTERS

- A very smooth yarn can be created from the fleece, with an almost silk-like quality. When finely spun, it can produce lightweight knitwear. Teeswater yarn is perfect for creating textures like Aran and moss stitch as it gives high definition.
- The wool, when knitted up, has good drape with a sleek, shiny finish.
- Durable yet soft to handle, it doesn't readily felt, so can be machine washed.
- With a long staple length, the fleece should be worsted spun.

Suitable alternatives are the Wensleydale, Cotswold, or Masham.

Wensleydale

This is a large-framed sheep that can weigh up to 135kg (300lb). It has blue-grey colouring on its face and legs. The impressively long, curly fleece will reach the ground within a year if left untouched. Heavy ringlets hang in individual locks from the body, making the breed's appearance distinctive. Even the forelock – which covers an otherwise wool-free face – is long and coiled.

The Wensleydale emerged in the 19th century in North Yorkshire. It can be traced back to a Dishley Leicester ram called Bluecap, born in 1839 and crossed with a local Teeswater longwool ewe (sadly, her name wasn't recorded).

Wool Characteristics

- Wensleydale is one of the finest longwools. The fleece ranges from dark to light, including dark grey, russet brown, and soft white. It yields a strong yet soft yarn, and its lustrous quality makes it excellent for blending with other fibres like cotton and linen.
- Staple length: 15-30cm (6-11¾in)
- Weight of fleece: 3-7kg (6.6-15lb)

TIPS FOR SPINNERS AND KNITTERS

- The wool has a great texture and can look a bit hairy – almost like a mohair-type yarn – so is excellent for merging colours in pattern knitting.
- It's a particularly popular wool with hand spinners and knitters due to its ease of spinning and attractive look.
- When spun by hand it has a lovely irregular, bobbly appearance.
- Wenselydale is one of the easiest pure breed knitting yarns to find as many larger-scale spinners produce it.
- Needs to be worsted spun due to its staple length.

Suitable alternatives are the Leicester Longwool, Wensleydale, British Milk Sheep, or Masham.

The Longwools

The Downs and Shortwools

Cheviot

This is a compact hill sheep with a white face and a distinctive ruff behind the ears. Rams can have horns. Developed in the 14th century, it's said to have been running in the Cheviot hills (between Northumberland and the Scottish border) since records began. The Cheviot is sometimes referred to as the South Country Cheviot, even though it's from the Scottish border region. Within the Cheviot family there are also the larger North Country Cheviot and the Brecknock Hill Cheviot.

Alert and active, the Cheviot is often used in sheepdog training. It has one of the largest populations of pure breed sheep.

Wool Characteristics

- The fleece produces an exceptionally fine, crisp wool with a soft handle.
- Staple length: 8-12cm (3-4¾in)
- Weight of fleece: 2-3kg (4.4-6.6lb)

TIPS FOR SPINNERS AND KNITTERS

- Because of its shorter staple, the fleece produces a fluffy yarn, similar to the Shetland.
- There is a smooth, matt quality to the wool; it's versatile and durable. This is an easy yarn to knit with, meaning it's good for beginners.
- As there are naturally white and black fleeces, a good range of white to dark browns are available as yarns: this makes it a good choice for intasia and Fair Isle knitwear.
- Its short staple means it should be woollen spun.

A suitable alternative is the Portland.

Dorset Down

A stocky, powerfully built, barrel-shaped sheep, the Dorset Down has a dense, springy fleece, with a black face and ears.

The breed is found mainly in the Southwest of England and is one of the oldest breeds of native sheep in Britain. It was developed in the early 1800s by crossing local Wiltshire, Buckinghamshire, and Hampshire ewes with South Down rams, making them ideally suited to the local area. The breed society was registered in 1904, making it one of the earliest.

A relatively calm sheep, the Dorset Down is a year-round prolific breeder, known as the "king of the prime-lamb breeds". The rams are virile, with – according to the Rare Breeds Survival Trust – "one ram covering 20 ewes in a 24-hour period".

Despite this, the breed is at risk.

Wool Characteristics

- The white fleece has a touch of cream and produces a crisp, springy yarn.
- Staple length: 5–8cm (2–3in)
- Weight of fleece: 2.25–3kg (5–6.6lb)

TIPS FOR SPINNERS AND KNITTERS

- If graded carefully it can produce a good knitting yarn, especially for knitting textures, but is better for outerwear.
- Excellent for socks and hats.
- The fleece is ideal for stuffing padded items like gilets, as it makes them exceptionally warm.
- Great for hand spinning as the fleece is easy to handle.
- With a short staple length, the fleece should be woollen spun.

Suitable alternatives are the Hampshire or Southdown.

The Downs and Shortwools

Dorset Down • 45

The Downs and Shortwools

Hampshire Down

The large, block-shaped Hampshire Down is hornless with a brown nose and dark brown ears that curve slightly backwards.

It was established by cross-breeding the Wiltshire, Hampshire, and Berkshire. This has resulted in a sheep that adapts well to different environments, and is a superior mutton breed, noted for its early maturity.

The Hampshire Down is one of the most common of the pure breeds and is found worldwide. Nonetheless, it remains at risk.

Wool Characteristics

- The fine, dense white fleece has a springy texture and great elasticity, producing wool with a reasonably soft handle and good durability.
- Staple length: 5–8cm (2–3in)
- Weight of fleece: 2.25–3kg (5–6.6lb)

TIPS FOR SPINNERS AND KNITTERS

- This is excellent for Fair Isle knitting – The Grey Sheep Co. on the south coast of Britain specializes in producing the wool in a wonderful variety of colours (see Sourcing Guide).
- Like many of these fleece types, it benefits from being loose spun as this makes the wool softer.
- The wool is good for sweaters, cardigans, and accessories.
- As it doesn't felt well, it's good for machine washing.

Suitable alternatives are the Dorset or South Down.

Llanwenog

This medium-sized breed has a black face and a tuft on the forehead. It's a descendant of the Roman longwool.

The Llanwenog was developed in West Wales in the late 19th century from a Shropshire crossed with a now-extinct black-faced breed called the Llanllwni.

The breed is kept primarily for meat. It has a placid temperament, is not prone to escaping, and can be housed in winter. Ewes are known for their good mothering and produce lots of twins and triplets.

This is an at-risk breed.

Wool Characteristics

- The Llanwenog has a stone-coloured fleece with a splendid lustre. The longer fleeces can be combed to keep the natural sheen of the fibre. A wavy crimp gives the wool texture.
- Staple length: 6–10cm (2½–4in)
- Weight of fleece: 2–2.5kg (4.4–5.5lb)

TIPS FOR SPINNERS AND KNITTERS

- Great for cardigans and outerwear. It's very similar to the Lleyn, just with a little more lustre.
- The shiny fleece is popular with textile artists.
- It's also a favourite with hand spinners as its wavy crimp makes it excellent to handle.
- With a medium staple length, the fleece can be woollen or worsted spun. Worsted spinning maintains the natural lustre and sleekness.

Suitable alternatives are the Lleyn or Romney.

The Downs and Shortwools

The Downs and Shortwools

Lleyn

This medium-sized, hornless sheep has a white face and head. There's no wool on the ears or legs.

The breed is native to the Lleyn Peninsular, a headland on the northwest coast of Wales, where it's said to have been imported by a wealthy landlord during the 19th century to improve the meat of local Welsh stock.

Lleyns are renowned for being easy to manage and are found widely throughout the UK. King Charles III keeps a flock near his Highgrove Estate in Gloucestershire.

Wool Characteristics

- The fleece is pure cream and creates a strong, sturdy fibre.
- Staple length: 6–12cm (2½–4¾in)
- Weight of fleece: 2.5–3.5 kg (5.5–7.7lb)

TIPS FOR SPINNERS AND KNITTERS

- With careful selection, using the first cut from the lamb (usually the softest fleece) you can get yarn that makes a great cardigan. The coarser fibres can be quite hairy, producing yarns with interesting textures.
- The yarn is ideal for weaving.
- Sturdy fibres mean that this is a good option for knitting warm everyday garments like jackets, as well as being suitable for household textiles such as table mats or knitted stools.
- With a medium staple length, the fleece can be woollen or worsted spun.

Suitable alternatives are the Dorset Down or Hampshire Down.

48 • Lleyn

Norfolk Horn

This feisty, medium-sized hardy sheep has a black face, and long body and legs. It's alert-looking with strong, open spiral horns.

Established in the 13th century, it's one of Britain's oldest breeds. It was developed in East Anglia out of an old Saxon black-faced sheep from the time of the Viking invasion. The breed has the ability to graze heathlands and the poorest soils. This feature alone makes it a valuable sheep worth fighting to save.

The breed became functionally extinct in the 1970s when the last pure-bred ram died, followed by the last ewe. Before their demise, one of the Norfolk Horn derivative breeds, the Suffolk, was used in an effort to salvage as much of the original genetics as possible. The resulting sheep became the current Norfolk Horn – meaning it isn't the original pure breed. It remains at risk.

Wool Characteristics

- The fleece is light and lofty, with a soft crimp, producing yarn with character and elasticity. White, with a hint of grey in adults, whereas the lambs are often darker or mottled.
- Staple length: 7-10cm (2¾-4in)
- Weight of fleece: 1.5-1.75kg (3.3-3.9kg)

TIPS FOR SPINNERS AND KNITTERS

- The wool offers a balance of softness and durability, although is probably not suitable for wearing next to the skin.
- Best for sturdy, practical projects like socks, outerwear, bags, and mittens.
- Produces a warm and resilient knit with good stitch definition.
- Great for Nordic patterns and textured stitches such as cable. Also good for felting projects.
- With a short staple length, the fleece should be woollen spun.

Suitable alternatives are the Oxford Down or Hampshire Down.

The Downs and Shortwools

The Downs and Shortwools

Oxford Down

This breed has a black face and side-set black ears. Heavy wool on the forelock and cheeks can encircle the eyes like a mask.

These gentle giants were developed in the 19th century and are the second largest and heaviest of the British downland sheep. They were bred by crossing Cotswold rams with Hampshire and South Down ewes. Oxford Downs produce a good quantity of fine fleece, which is soft and short with consistent, defined crimp.

In recent years, breeding for meat has been prioritised at the cost of wool quality. However, carefully selected fleeces can yield premium yarns that are soft enough for next-to-skin garments.

This is an at-risk breed.

Wool Characteristics

- The fleece is creamy matt white and heavy. It's lofty and springy with a moderate crimp.
- Staple length: 6–10cm (2½–4in)
- Weight of fleece: 2.5–3.5 kg (5.5–7.7lb)

TIPS FOR SPINNERS AND KNITTERS

- A practical fibre with excellent resilience and warmth, it's good for outer garments and holds its shape well. While it lacks the softness of finer wools, it offers durability and elasticity.
- The fleece can contain a fair amount of lanolin, so hand wash thoroughly before spinning.
- Due to its reluctance to felt, it's suitable for machine washing.
- The wool blends beautifully with finer fibres like mohair, which add lustre and strength.
- With a short staple length, the fleece should be woollen spun.

Suitable alternatives are the South Down or Hampshire Down.

Ryeland

Compact, robust, and adaptable, the Ryeland has a heavily woolled face and legs (like a huge teddy bear), and no horns.

One of Britain's oldest sheep breeds, dating from the Middle Ages, it was developed by the monks of Lemstore near Hereford more than 800 years ago. For a time, it produced one of the softest wools in the world – supposedly as soft as Spanish merino. Later breeding for improved meat production resulted in coarser fibre.

The Ryeland is characterful and pleasingly docile, essentially a labrador in sheep's clothing. It's a breed with a tight-knit flocking mentality.

Ryelands can be found in New Zealand and Australia – the latter sharing a similar quality of wool to Ryelands in the UK.

Wool Characteristics

- It has exceptionally soft, fluffy, and dense fleece with a springy handle.
- White Ryeland wool is pure while, while Coloured Ryeland fleeces can be shades of brown, grey, or near-black, often with fading at the tips.
- Staple length: 5-13cm (2-5in)
- Weight of fleece: 2-3kg (4.4-6.6lb)

TIPS FOR SPINNERS AND KNITTERS

- Contacting the Ryeland Flock Book Society is the best way to source the softest fleeces. The Society is working on improving the wool.
- Its soft handle, good crimp, and elasticity contribute to a smooth and springy yarn, so it's popular with spinners.
- Its elasticity makes it perfect for fitted items like hats, gloves, and socks. Resistance to pilling means it's good for frequent-wear items.
- Works beautifully in textured knits like cable and lace.
- With a short staple length, the fleece should be woollen spun.

Suitable alternatives are the South Down or Cheviot.

The Downs and Shortwools

The Downs and Shortwools

Shropshire

This classic down-type sheep has a black nose and ears, short legs, and a barrel-shaped body.

Originally developed in the early 19th century in Shropshire and the West Midlands, its association was formed in 1882 and is the oldest breed society in the UK. The sheep thrive in a wide range of conditions.

In the 1930s, Shropshires were the most common breed in North America.

The ewes are good mothers to their vigorous, fast-growing lambs. This is an at-risk breed.

Wool Characteristics

- The resilient white fleece is a good all-rounder. The wool is springy, thanks to the crimp of the staple, so has good elasticity.
- Consistent quality makes it ideal for spinning and weaving.
- Staple length: 6–15cm (2½–6in)
- Weight of fleece: 2–3 kg (4.4–6.6lb)

TIPS FOR SPINNERS AND KNITTERS

- The finer fleeces produce a durable yarn that can be worn next to the skin.
- Coarser grades are excellent for hats, mittens, socks, and sweaters.
- Fleece is low in lanolin so washing is straightforward.
- The wool blends beautifully with silk or alpaca for added drape and softness.
- Its spring makes it ideal for ribbing and fitted designs and it retains its shape well.
- Works beautifully with textures as it offers excellent stitch definition.
- With a variable staple length, the fleece can be worsted or woollen spun.

Suitable alternatives are the South Down or Dorset Down.

South Down

Docile and affectionate, the South Down has an unusual triangular-shaped furry face and small ears. It has short legs and a stocky body.

The breed was established in the 17th century to roam the Sussex Downs, then improved a century later. This is the source from which all other down breeds originate. Some historians believe that these were also the first sheep to be exported to America.

When bred in the particularly rainy Tamar Valley in Cornwall, South Downs occasionally develop algae in their fleece!

Their meat is unequalled in tenderness and flavour which, combined with the popularity of their wool, means they're one of the few rare breeds that's thriving.

Wool Characteristics

- The fleece produces versatile, resilient and medium-grade wool in terms of its softness. It's extremely dense with fine strands. With careful sorting, the South Down has the potential to produce the finest wool of all the down sheep.
- Weight of fleece: 1.5–2kg (3.3–4.4kg)
- Staple length: 4–6cm (1½–2½in)

TIPS FOR SPINNERS AND KNITTERS

- The wool's springiness means it's used to make wool duvets and mattresses; this makes the fleece and yarn hard to find for knitting.
- The wool doesn't felt, so is machine washable.
- Elasticity makes it ideal for socks, mittens, and hats. Its soft texture also makes it suitable for next-to-the skin items, such as baby clothes or cowls.
- Apply a slightly higher twist when spinning to prevent the short fibres from splitting apart.
- With a short staple length, the fleece should be woollen spun.

Suitable alternatives are the Cheviot or Shropshire.

The Downs and Shortwools

South Down • 53

THE PROJECTS

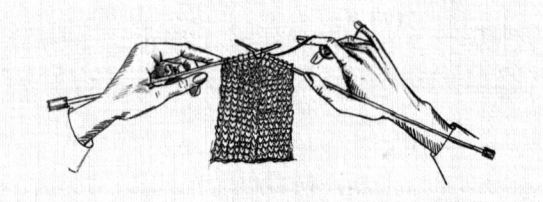

Wensleydale Longwool
Furgus Unisex Jumper

Leicester Longwool
Cola Gillet

Border Leicester
Moina Sweater

Bluefaced Leicester
Carril Fair Isle Jumper

Castlemilk Moorit
Tara Cardigan

Jacob
Atha Checkered Hat

Romney
Semo Sweater

Portland
Malvina Shawl

Cheviot
Orla Paisley Intarsia Sweater

Black Welsh Mountain
Ullin Sweater

The names of the projects are inspired by The Poems of Ossian. *These epic poems are partly based on Gaelic ballads, which recount the heroic deeds of the third-century warrior-bard Ossian.*

Tools, Materials, and Sizing

When starting any knitting project, you'll want to ensure that the time you invest will be rewarded by the creation of something you can wear with pride and treasure for many years.

There are many tempting options when it comes to buying equipment, but you don't need them all. While some items are essential, others will simply save you time if your budget allows.

Hank Winder

Your heritage wool will be sold as hanks or balls. Hanks (also known as skeins) have become increasingly popular, particularly among artisan producers – possibly because they're easier to wind and display.

If you buy your wool in hanks, you'll need to convert it into balls before starting your project. To do this, undo the ties, pop the hank over your knees or a chairback and manually wind the yarn into a ball. If you're embarking on a bigger project, you might want to use a hank winder (also known as a yarn swift). Here, you simply pop the hank onto the winder, open it up with the umbrella-like mechanism, and either manually create a ball or use a ball winder (see below).

Ball Winder (Yarn Winder)

This tool allows you to quickly transfer your wool from the hank winder into (slightly square-shaped) balls of wool known as "cakes". These cakes are much neater and easier to store and if they're wound correctly you should have a visible central strand of wool that's easily accessible when you start knitting. The cake's shape means it's less likely than a round ball to roll away as you draw the yarn during knitting. For projects requiring two strands of the same wool – which several in this book do – you can use both ends of one ball instead of two balls.

56 · Tools, Materials, and Sizing

Straight Needles

When it comes to needles, there's a huge variety to choose from, and what you pick depends on your knitting style and the pattern you've chosen to knit. If you like to work with one needle under your arm, you'll need two straight needles. If you prefer knitting in the European style, then choose circular needles (see below).

While needles are available in plastic, metal and wood, the latter two materials are best for sustainability. Plastic needles can also be quite bendy and sometimes catch the yarn.

Needles are usually 25cm to 38cm (10in to 15in) long with sizes ranging from very thin (1mm) to very thick (20mm). It's considered easier to start with straight needles, then move on to circular needles as you become a more experienced knitter.

Wooden needles come in different price ranges, starting with those made from bamboo. These are perfectly satisfactory as they provide some resistance, meaning they keep the stitches on the needle but are still smooth enough not to catch the yarn.

If you want to treat yourself to a more premium product, there are birch and rosewood needles. Some knitters prefer wood as they are warmer to handle than metal and feel more solid than bamboo. Although both bamboo and wood will snap if you accidentally sit on them!

Metal needles have the advantage of lasting for a long time; many having been passed down through the generations. You can pick them up cheaply in charity shops, but even buying them new is inexpensive. Metal needles have a smoother finish compared to most wooden ones, so the stitches can slip off easily. This is great if you are a quick knitter, but they can be too slippery for silk or some of the longwool yarns used for the projects in this book.

Circular Needles

These are made of two smaller pointed needles connected by a fine, flexible plastic cable. They're called "circular" because they allow you to knit in a continuous round. You can find various lengths to suit your pattern, typically from 40cm to 152cm (16in to 60in). Different needle sizes are available, just like straight needles.

Circular needles have become more popular over the past few years due to their versatility. Not only can you use them to knit in the round (as more modern knitting designs and traditional Nordic garments call for) but also for flat knitting. The weight of the knitting is distributed across not just the needles but also the flexible cable, which alleviates strain on the knitter's arms and shoulders. It's arguably faster to knit stocking stitch this way as there's no need for purling when knitting in the round. Needle heads are available in wood or metal but the circular connecting cable is generally made from plastic.

Make sure the stitches aren't twisted around the cable when you're casting on and knitting the first few rows. The joy of this style of knitting is that there are no seams to make up after finishing your project, which may be another of the reasons people like knitting with this style of needle.

Interchangeable circular needles are available in box sets containing separate needle tips and cables in a variety of sizes and lengths. This means you have the advantage of being able to change needle size mid-project, which is particularly handy for required variations in tension (gauge).

Fixed circular needles come in the same standard widths as straight needles and are available in a selection of cable lengths. If you only need one or two needle sizes for your project, there's no need to invest in a full set of sizes. Like straight needles, second-hand circular needles can often be found in charity shops. Buying them is a good way to knit sustainably.

Double-pointed needles (DPNs) are available in both wood and metal. They're often sold in sets of 4 or 5 and are usually between 12cm and 20cm (5in and 8in) long. These are useful for smaller items that require circular knitting, such as socks, mittens, and hats. Some knitters prefer them to circular needles when knitting narrow sleeves.

Cable needles are small double-ended needles, usually 10cm (4in) long and 3mm to 4mm wide. They don't need to be the same width as the main knitting needles you're working with as the cable needle only holds the stitches while you cable. However, it's advisable not to choose cable needles that are wider than your knitting needles as they may stretch the stitch during transferal.

Stitch Markers

These small hoops are used mostly in circular knitting to mark the beginning and end of a round. They can be simple, tubular 'end of each row' types, or small table-top devices that you move on as you knit. They can show where you'll need to change to a new texture or cable pattern, or they can mark sections of a more complicated knit. It's easy to create your own stitch markers by making a loop from a contrast colour yarn – saving you the need to buy them.

Lockable stitch markers can be opened and closed (like a safety pin or lobster clasp) to attach to your knitting. Usually made from plastic or metal, these are useful for marking rows that need a decrease/increase in stitches, or if you're counting a specific number of rows. This cuts out the need to keep counting up from the hem.

Row Counters

These are simple, tubular, rotating devices. They sit at the end of your needle, and you move the marker on at the end of each row. There are also row counting apps that you can use on your smart phone. These are particularly helpful if you have multiple projects on the go.

Tension Square Measures

Ensuring your tension (gauge) is correct in relation to your pattern is always important to achieve a correct fit. It's even more so when you're working with artisan yarns that aren't always a consistent thickness (see Working With Heritage Wool). There are various tools that help with measuring, for instance the one illustrated has a 10cm (4in) window at its middle that you can use to count rows and stitches. Of course, you can simply use a ruler for the job, but this tool helps keep the knitting flat while you're counting.

Scissors

Any type of scissors will cut through yarn, although a smaller size is easier to work with. Mini sheep shears (also known as thread snips) are perfect for snipping the ends of the yarn – and feel particularly fitting!

Tapestry / Darning Needle

You'll need a medium to large tapestry needle to sew up your garment after knitting and to mend any holes. A needle with a larger eye is perfect for threading chunky yarns. Make sure the tip of the needle is blunt, so it goes between the stitches rather than through the yarn.

Latch Needles

Latch needles are very useful for picking up dropped stitches. The hinged latch mechanism at the end of the needle opens and shuts to lock in the dropped stitch, making it easy to pick it up and thread back to the top. A crochet hook would work too, but the latch helps to keep the stitch inside the hook.

A Note About Sizing

Where a pattern in this book is written for multiple sizes, stitch counts and measurements will vary for the different sizes. In this instance, the first number given is for the smallest size and subsequent numbers in brackets are for larger sizes, in order. If only one stitch count or measurement is given, it applies to all sizes.

Working With Heritage Wool

Native-breed sheep's wool is different to commercial wool – the former is produced in small batches, while the latter is spun in high volumes for a consistent finish. The production and refinement of rare-breed wool is an area that's still evolving, as sheep have, in recent generations, been bred for meat rather than their fleeces. It's possible to buy whole fleeces from farmers and wash and spin it yourself. However, the following assumes that you have purchased skeins of spun wool.

Not all Skeins are the Same

You'll find that each skein has unique characteristics – and the fact that they are not uniform is part of their charm. One challenge is the consistency of the thickness of the wool. Most commercially bought hand-knitting wool conforms to five different weight classifications: lace weight, four-ply, DK, aran, and chunky. Meaning, for instance, a DK weight is the same from one manufacturer to another.

With rare breeds, the fleeces are processed by small, artisan mills who don't all produce skeins to the same weight or thickness. Therefore, it's vital that you knit a tension (gauge) swatch before starting any project so that you can adjust the pattern accordingly. A swatch measuring 10cm x 10cm (4in x 4in) is the perfect size for any project. Once finished, always wash the swatch. The yarn will likely bloom and soften, altering the gauge slightly.

A Taste of the Country

Farmers have different methods of husbandry. Some keep their sheep out on the hills for most of the year, while others put them in barns for the colder spells. Either way, there will often be tiny bits of vegetation or bedding left in the wool, even after it's gone through the spinning process. Again, artisan spinning is very different to commercial spinning on huge machines. Personally, I like finding a bit of straw or moss in my wool as it reminds me of its provenance, and it's easy to remove with a pair of tweezers.

Give it a Wash

Although fleeces are washed before spinning to remove lanolin, vegetable oil may be used during the spinning process to make it easier. If you buy your skeins of wool direct from a farmer, it's quite likely that they won't have washed it to remove all of the oil. This is something you'll need to do when you've completed your garment. It will mean that the wool is slightly rougher to knit, but when you wash the article once knitted, it will become softer. I would advise that you first give the piece a good soak for two or three hours, in warm, soapy water (I use a mild detergent or wool wash). Then gently agitate it to remove any excess oils before rinsing thoroughly.

If You Love it, Buy a Lot!

Very few native and rare breed wools are commercially produced, meaning that most are made in small batches. These vary from spinner to spinner but also (a bit like wine) from year to year. Sheep are living creatures, and their wool is affected by things like their age and environment. A wet, cool summer, or a hot dry one will produce different handles to the fleece. Sickness, or traumatic events such as dog attacks, can again cause the fleeces to have a different handle or weak spots. Therefore, when you find a great yarn make sure you buy enough to finish your project, as the next lot you buy could be quite different.

Left: Skeins of wool from the British Milk sheep, one of Britain's rarest breeds. Thanks to George and Sara Wood, who own the Arden and Aspley flock, for their help in developing this fine wool.

The Feel of Rare Wool

The three rare breed wool types – longwool, primitive, and shortwool – have different characteristics that make them look and feel distinctive. When it comes to knitting, you'll notice these differences immediately.

Longwool fleece has a slightly slippery hand feel, which can make knitting trickier. You might want to use wooden needles instead of metal. The wool has a heavy feel and drapes well when knitted as garments, which is something to consider when choosing your pattern.

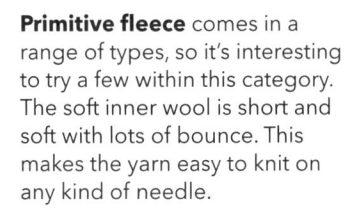

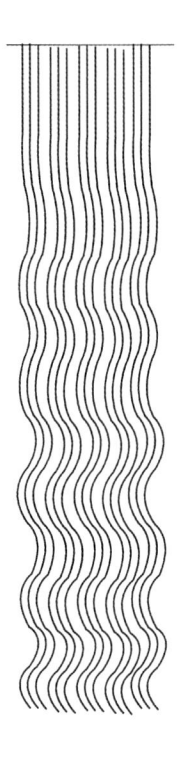

Primitive fleece comes in a range of types, so it's interesting to try a few within this category. The soft inner wool is short and soft with lots of bounce. This makes the yarn easy to knit on any kind of needle.

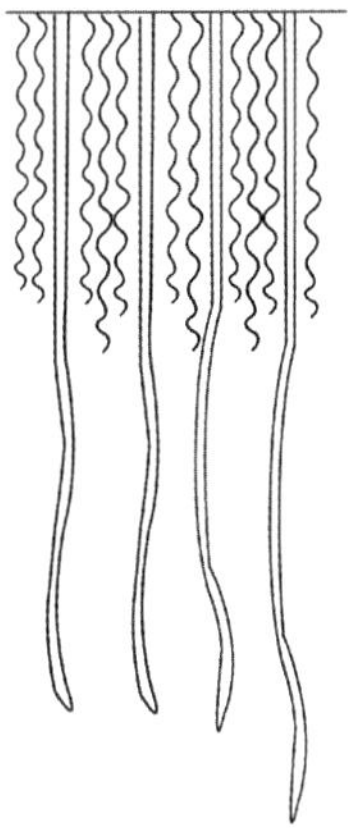

Shortwool fleece has lots of crimp, which gives the yarn a bouncy handle. This wool is comfortable to hand knit, as it holds well onto the needles and its springiness makes cabling easy.

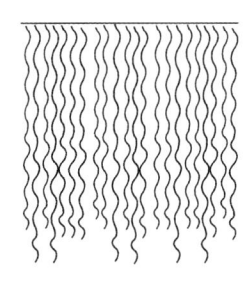

Longwool fleeces contain continuous fine strands with a consistent curl from root to tip.

Primitive fleeces combine coarse kemp and shorter, fine underwool.

Fleeces from down or shortwool sheep are made up of crimpy fibres of consistent lengths.

Sheep Societies

One of the lovely things about pure breed sheep is that each has its own breed society working to maintain the breed's heritage, health, and commercial viability. Societies vary in terms of size and remit, but many are able to provide yarn or give contact details of farmers who produce it (see Sourcing Guide).

The North Country Cheviot Sheep Society, for instance, is particularly well-organized, with members all over the UK. It has an interactive website where you can find the flock closest to where you live. When I phoned a farmer in Surrey, he'd just done his shearing and invited me to visit. On the day, he gave me a fascinating tour of his farm, then handed me a bag of very fine fleece.

For a list of sheep societies whose breeds are featured in this book, go to www.bookmarkedhub.com.

Working With Heritage Wool • 61

Wensleydale sheep produce one of the most distinctive and prized types of wool. Its silky lustre combines with a hairy loft (rather like mohair) and it drapes beautifully. The Furgus unisex jumper is an easy, everyday style, so I wanted a durable yarn that's also pleasurable to wear. Colours range from warm white and light grey to dark brown, and working two together produces a soft melange effect. This is a look that feels both natural and luxurious.

Furgus Unisex Jumper
in Wensleydale Longwool

Pattern Notes

Furgus is a simple, classic style and is designed as a gender-neutral garment. The simple pattern uses only two stitches – knit and purl – so it's ideal for beginners. Construction is flat, bottom up with drop shoulders. The rolled neckline is worked in the round.

The trims, hem, and cuffs are knitted in a chunky 2x2 rib. If preferred, they can be knitted in stocking stitch to match the body. The version pictured follows this variation.

The pattern is written for five sizes: small, medium, large, X-large, and XX-large.

Skill level: for beginners through to experienced knitters

Materials

YARN
Wensleydale 4-ply Marl Wool (100% Wensleydale wool), 4-ply, 50g (170m/186yds). Supplied by Wensleydale Longwool Sheep Shop

Shade: Natural; 700 (750) (800) (850) (900)g; 14 (15) (16) (17) (18) balls with 2 strands held together throughout

NEEDLES
- 4mm (US 6)
- 3.25mm (US 3) 40cm or 60cm (16in or 24in) circular needles or DPNs, used for neckline

OTHER
- Stitch holder

Tension (Gauge)

20 sts x 26 rows measures 10cm (4in) square over stocking stitch using 4mm (US 6) needles.

Sizes and Garment Measurements

(Measurements after blocking)

	SMALL	MEDIUM	LARGE	X-LARGE	XX-LARGE
To fit bust	81–86cm (32–34in)	92–97cm (36–38in)	102–107cm (40–42in)	112–117cm (44–46in)	122–127cm (48–50in)
Bust circumference	102cm (40in)	112cm (44in)	122cm (48in)	132cm (52in)	142cm (56in)
Length from hem to underarm	38cm (15in)	38cm (15in)	38cm (15in)	39cm (15¼in)	39cm (15¼in)
Length from hem to upper shoulder	64cm (25in)	65cm (25½in)	66cm (26in)	67cm (26½in)	67cm (26½in)
Depth of armhole	23cm (9in)	24cm (9½in)	25cm (10in)	25cm (10in)	25cm (10in)
Sleeve length from cuff to underarm (men)	59cm (23¼in)	60cm (23½in)	61cm (24in)	62cm (24½in)	62cm (24½in)
Sleeve length from cuff to underarm (women)	46cm (18in)	47cm (18½in)	48cm (19in)	49cm (19¼in)	49cm (19¼in)
Upper sleeve circumference	43cm (17in)	44cm (17¼in)	45cm (17¾in)	46cm (18in)	47cm (18½in)

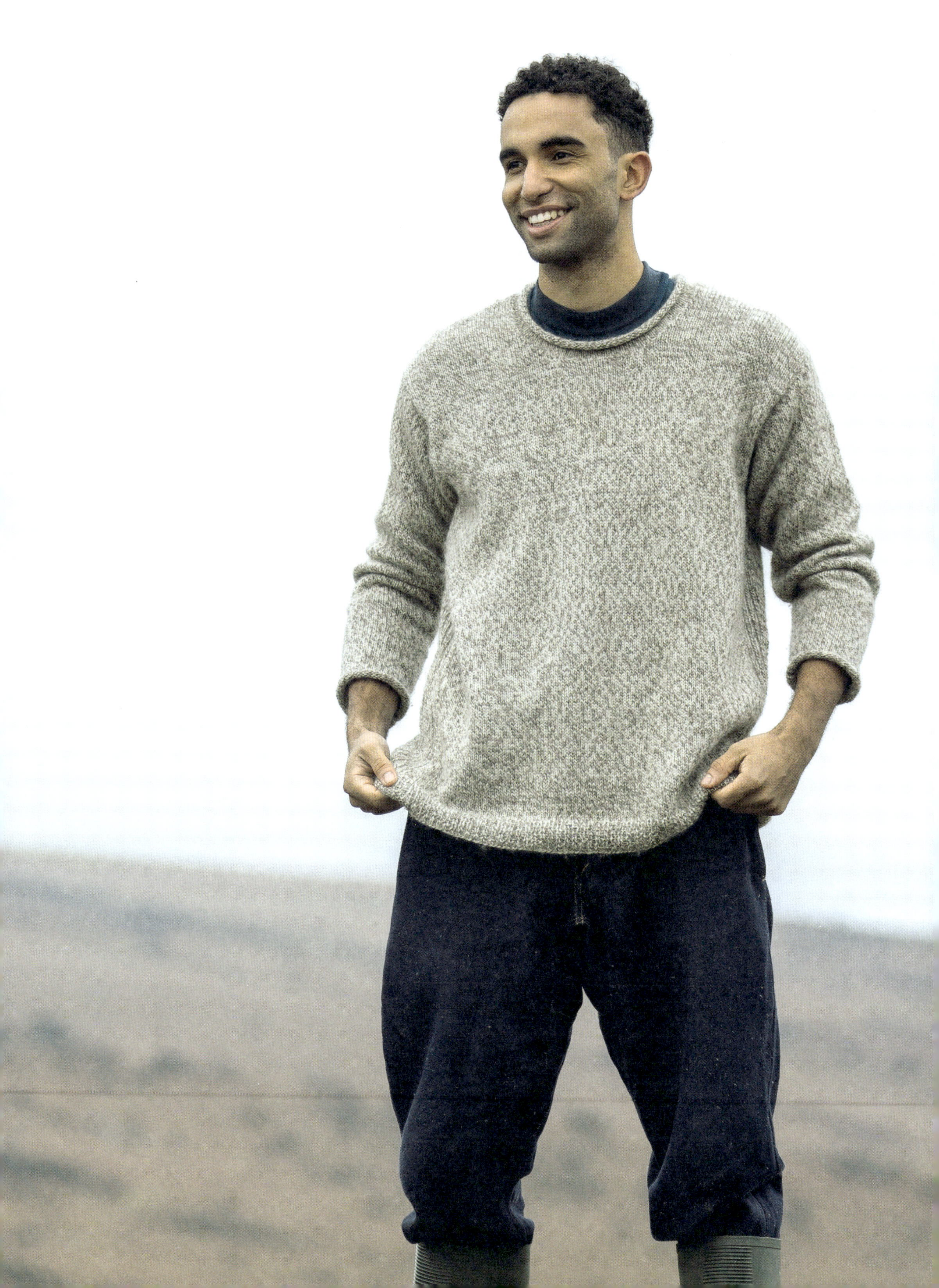

Instructions

Back

**Using 4mm (US 6) needles and with 2 strands held together throughout, cast on 102 (114) (122) (134) (142) sts.

Rib row 1 (RS): K2, [p2, k2] to end.

Rib row 2 (WS): P2, [k2, p2] to end.

Rep above 2 rows until work measures 6cm (2½in), ending on a WS row.

FOR SIZES M, XL ONLY:

Dec by 2 sts as follows:

Next row (RS): K10, k2tog, k up to last 11 sts, ssk, k to end.

Next row (WS): P to end. (-- (112) (--) (132) (--) sts)

FOR ALL SIZES:

Starting with k row, work in ss until work measures 38 (38) (38) (39) (39)cm (15 (15) (15) (15¼) (15¼)in) from cast on edge ending on a WS row.

Armhole shaping

Cast (bind) off 4 (4) (5) (6) (6) sts at beg of next 2 rows.

Dec row (RS): K1, k2tog, k to last 3 sts, ssk, k1.

Next row (WS): P to end.

Dec by rep the last 2 rows 2 (3) (3) (3) (4) times more. (88 (96) (104) (112) (120) sts)**

Cont in ss until work measures 61 (62) (63) (64) (64)cm (24 (24½) (24¾) (25) (25)in) from cast on edge, ending on WS row.

Shoulder shaping

Cast (bind) off 5 (6) (7) (8) (9) sts in the next 2 rows. (78 (84) (90) (96) (102) sts)

Cast (bind) off 6 (6) (7) (8) (9) sts in the next 2 rows. (66 (72) (76) (80) (84) sts)

Cast (bind) off 6 (7) (8) (8) (9) sts in the next 2 rows. (54 (58) (60) (64) (66) sts)

Cast (bind) off 6 (7) (8) (9) (10) sts in the next 2 rows. (42 (44) (44) (46) (46) sts)

Cast (bind) off rem sts.

Front

Work as given for Back from ** to **.

Cont in ss until work measures 53 (54) (55) (55) (55)cm (21 (21¼) (21½) (21½) (21½)in) from cast on edge, ending on a WS row.

Neckline shaping

Next row (RS): K36 (39) (43) (47) (51), turn, leaving the rem sts on a st holder.

Work each side of neck separately, as follows:

Using one of below dec row instructions depending on RS or WS row, dec 1 st on neckline edge on the next 9 (9) (9) (10) (10) rows, then on the next 3 alt rows, then on the following 4th row:

RS dec row: K to last 2 sts, ssk.

WS dec row: P2togtbl, p to end.

Number of rem sts for left shoulder is 23 (26) (30) (33) (37) sts.

Cont in ss until work measures 61 (62) (63) (64) (64)cm (24 (24½) (24¾) (25) (25)in) from cast on edge, ending on a WS row.

Left shoulder shaping

Next row (RS): Cast (bind) off 5 (6) (7) (8) (9) sts, work to end.

Next row (WS): P to end.

Next row: Cast (bind) off 6 (6) (7) (8) (9) sts, work to end.

Next row: P to end.

Next row: Cast (bind) off 6 (7) (8) (8) (9) sts, work to end.

Next row: P to end.

Next row: Cast (bind) off rem 6 (7) (8) (9) (10) sts.

Return to sts on holder, leave the neckline centre 16 (18) (18) (18) (18) sts on holder and transfer rem 36 (39) (43) (47) (51) sts to working needle.

With RS facing rejoin yarn, k to end.

Using one of below dec row instructions depending on RS or WS row, dec 1 st on neckline edge on the next 9 rows, then on the next 3 alt rows, then on following 4th row:

RS dec row: K2tog, k to end.

WS dec row: P to last 2 sts, p2tog.

Number of rem sts for left shoulder is 23 (26) (30) (33) (37) sts.

Cont in ss until work measures 61 (62) (63) (64) (64)cm (24 (24½) (24¾) (25) (25)in) from cast on edge, ending on a RS row.

66 · Furgus Unisex Jumper

Right shoulder shaping

Next row (WS): Cast (bind) off 5 (6) (7) (8) (9) sts, work to end.

Next row (RS): K to end.

Next row: Cast (bind) off 6 (6) (7) (8) (9) sts, work to end.

Next row: K to end.

Next row: Cast (bind) off 6 (7) (8) (8) (9) sts, work to end.

Next row: K to end.

Next row: Cast (bind) off rem 6 (7) (8) (9) (10) sts.

Sleeves (make 2)

Using 4mm (US 6) needles and with 2 strands together throughout, cast on 46 (46) (50) (50) (50) sts.

Work same rib as given for Back for 6cm (2½in), ending on a WS row.

WOMEN'S VERSION:

Starting with k row, work in ss, shaping sides by inc 1 st at each end of next and every following 4th row until there are 86 (88) (90) (92) (94) sts, ending on WS row, as follows: K2, M1L, k to last 2 sts, M1R, k2.

Continue in ss until work measures 46 (47) (48) (49) (49)cm (18 (18½) (19) (19¼) (19¼)in) ending on a WS row.

MEN'S VERSION:

Starting with k row, work in ss shaping sides by inc 1 st at each end of next and every following 4th row until there are 86 (88) (90) (92) (94) sts, ending on WS row, as follows: K2, M1L, k to last 2 sts, M1R, k2.

Continue in ss until work measures 59 (60) (61) (62) (62)cm (23¼ (23½) (24) (24½) (24½)in) ending on a WS row.

BOTH WOMEN'S & MEN'S VERSION:

Cast (bind) off 4 (4) (5) (5) (6) sts at beg of next 2 rows. (78 (80) (80) (82) (82) sts)

Dec row (RS): K1, k2tog, k to last 3 sts, ssk, k1. (76 (78) (78) (80) (80) sts)

Next row (WS): P to end.

Dec by rep the above 2 rows 2 (3) (3) (3) (4) times more. (72 (72) (72) (74) (72) sts)

Cast (bind) off.

Assembly and finishing

Join front and back shoulder seams by sewing using mattress stitch.

Sew sleeves into armholes using mattress stitch.

Sew side and sleeve seams using mattress stitch.

Neckband

With RS facing, using 3.25mm (US 3) needles and starting at left shoulder seam, pick up and knit 23 (24) (25) (26) (27) sts down the left side of neck, k the centre 16 (18) (18) (18) (18) sts from st holder, pick up and knit 23 (24) (25) (26) (27) sts up the right side of neck to the right shoulder seam, then pick up and knit 42 (44) (44) (46) (46) sts at the back neck, arriving back to starting point. (104 (110) (112) (116) (118) sts)

PM on the needle to denote BOR/EOR.

Work 8 rounds in ss, slipping st marker when encountered.

Cast (bind) off.

Weave in all ends.

Block for a professional finished look.

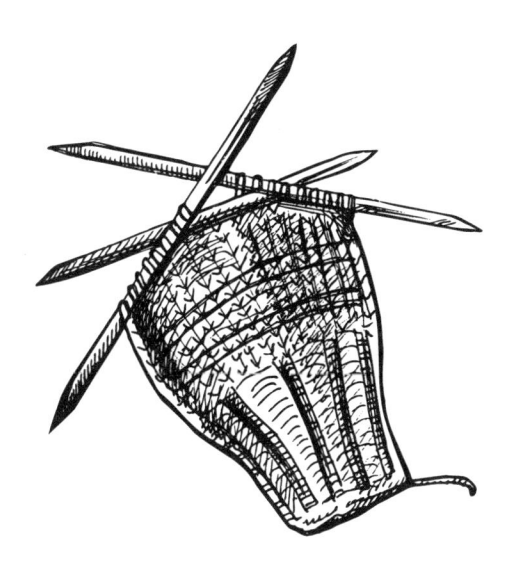

The Leicester Longwool is an ancient breed, and it's a joy to find this rare yarn produced with such a soft handle. The fact that the yarn is handspun creates a looser texture, making the most of the natural curl of the fleece. Despite its relatively smooth feel, this wool is still better used for outer garments. The Cola gilet (named after a Celtic king) works well as a trans-seasonal garment, providing a bit more style than the average cardigan!

Cola Gilet
in Leicester Longwool

Pattern Notes

The Cola gilet is a cropped boxy style with a simple yet elegant cable on each side of the front opening. The fit is oversized, making this a perfect complementary piece to slip over many outfits. It looks great worn with statement shirts, especially ones with wide sleeves.

There are no front fastenings, so the construction is straightforward. The pattern includes plain knit and purl stitches, and a simple cable.

The construction is flat bottom up. The shoulders are joined using decorative stitching called chain stitch (see Special Techniques).

The pattern is for five sizes: small, medium, large, X-large, and XX-large.

Skill level: for intermediate knitters

Materials

YARN

Leicester Longwool (100% wool), Aran, 100g (175m/191yds). Supplied by Pen-y-Lan Fibre Flock

Shade: Natural light grey; 400 (400) (450) (450) (500)g; 4 (4) (5) (5) (5) skeins

NEEDLES
- 4.5mm (US 7)
- Cable needle
- Tapestry needle

OTHER
- Stitch markers
- Stitch holder

Tension (Gauge)

18 sts x 25 rows measures 10cm (4in) square over stocking stitch using 4.5mm (US 7) needles.

Sizes and Garment Measurements

(Measurements after blocking)

	SMALL	MEDIUM	LARGE	X-LARGE	XX-LARGE
Back chest width	53cm (21in)	56cm (22in)	59cm (23¼in)	62cm (24½in)	66cm (26in)
Length from hem to upper shoulder	54cm (21¼in)	54cm (21¼in)	55cm (21½in)	56cm (22in)	57cm (22½in)
Length from hem to outer shoulder	42cm (16½in)	42cm (16½in)	43cm (17in)	43cm (17in)	44cm (17¼in)
Length from hem to under armhole	19cm (7½in)	19cm (7½in)	19cm (7½in)	19cm (7½in)	19cm (7½in)

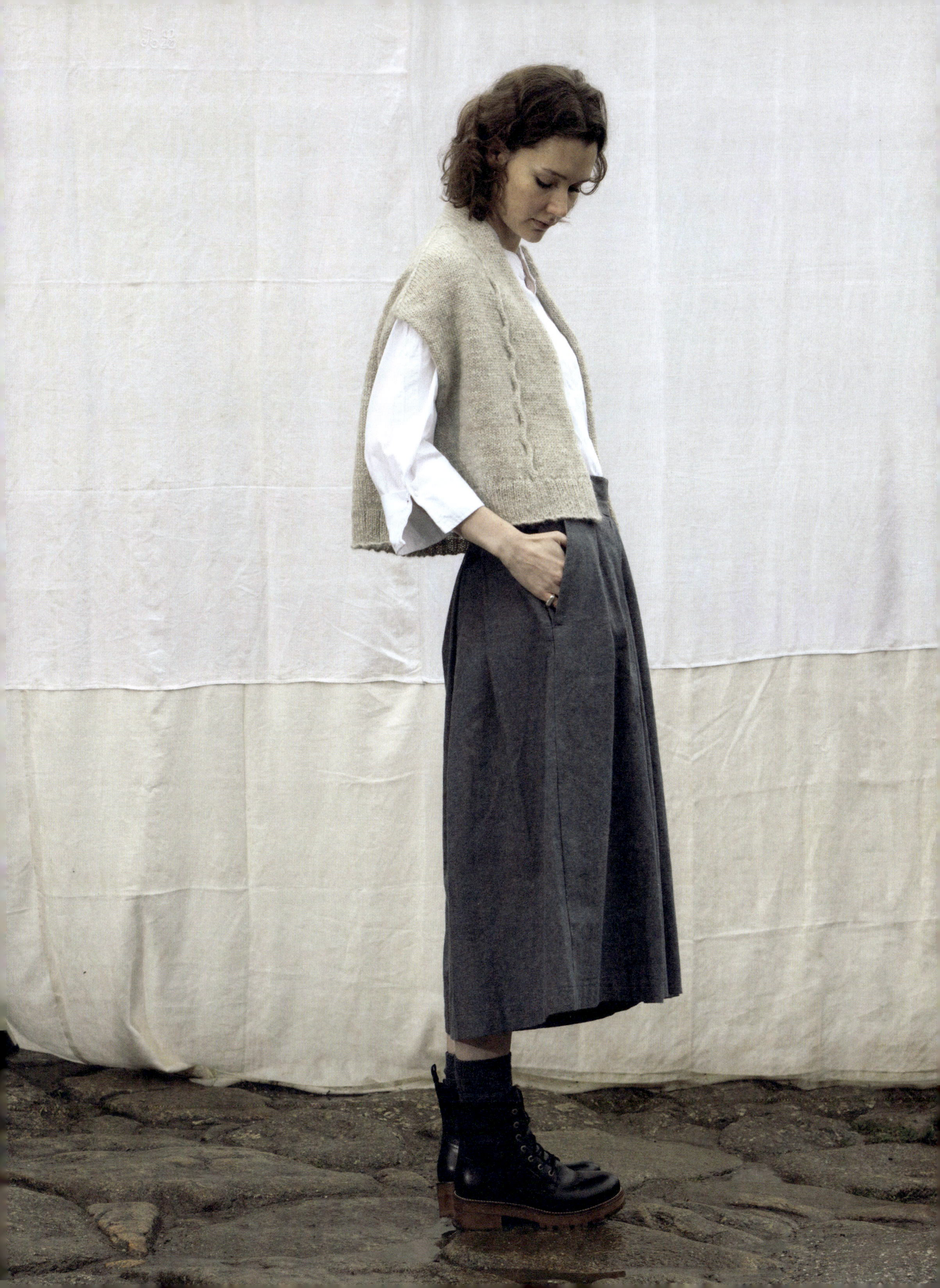

Instructions

Additional Notes

When knitting this wool, it's best to keep a looser tension (gauge) so as to make the most of the textured yarn.

The rib section of the gilet is knitted with the same needles as the body, as the rib section should be straight and not pull in, the wider 3 x 1 rib design should also help keep the hem flat.

I normally advocate machine washing, but as this wool is light, I recommend you hand wash this garment in cool water and dry flat.

Back

Cast on 91 (99) (107) (111) (119) sts.

Rib row 1 (RS): [K3, p1] to last 3 sts, k3.

Rib row 2 (WS): [P3, k1] to last 3 sts, p3.

Rep rib rows 1 and 2 seven times more.

Starting with knit row, work in ss until work measures 19cm (7½in) from cast on edge.

PM on first and last sts to mark beg of armholes.

Cont in ss until work measures 42 (42) (43) (43) (44)cm (16½ (16½) (17) (17) (17¼)in) from cast on edge, ending on WS row.

Shoulders and back neckline shaping

Next row (RS): K2togtbl, k to last 2 sts, k2tog. (89 (97) (105) (109) (117) sts)

Next row (WS): P2tog, p to last 2 sts, p2togtbl. (87 (95) (103) (107) (115) sts)

Rep above 2 rows 15 times more. (27 (35) (43) (47) (55) sts)

Next row (RS): K2togtbl, cast (bind) off 1 (5) (9) (10) (14) sts, k to last 2 sts, k2tog. 24 (28) (32) (35) (39) sts.

Next row (WS): P2tog, cast (bind) off 0 (4) (8) (9) (13) sts, p to end.

Cast (bind) off rem 23 (23) (23) (25) (25) sts representing back of neck.

Front left

Cast on 55 (59) (63) (67) (71) sts.

Rib row 1 (RS): [K3, p1] to last 3 sts, k3.

Rib row 2 (WS): [P3, k1] to last 3 sts, p3.

Rep rib rows 1 and 2 seven times more. On the last rib row inc at both ends of row as follows:

Rib row 16 (WS): P3, kfb, [p3, k1] to last 7 sts, p3, kfb, p3. (57 (61) (65) (69) (73) sts)

FL row 1 (RS): K30 (34) (38) (42) (46), PM, k6, p1, PM, k to end.

FL row 2 and all WS rows (WS): P to marker, SM, k1, p6, SM, p to end.

Note: Henceforth, unless specified otherwise, always SM whenever a st marker is encountered.

FL row 3: K to marker, C6B, p1, k to end.

FL row 5: K to marker, k6, p1, k to end.

FL row 7: As FL row 5.

FL row 9: K to marker, C6F, p1, k to end.

FL row 11: As FL row 5.

FL row 13: As FL row 5.

Last 12 rows (FL rows 3 to 14) define front left st pattern.

Cont in front left st pattern until work measures 19cm (7½in) from hem, ending on the WS row.

PM on first st of fabric to mark beg of armhole.

Cont in front left st pattern until work measures 42 (42) (43) (43) (44)cm (16½ (16½) (17) (17) (17¼)in) from hem, ending on a WS row.

Left shoulder shaping

Next row (RS): K2togtbl, work to end of row as per front left st pattern. (56 (60) (64) (68) (72) sts)

Next row (WS): Work as per front left st pattern to last 2 sts, p2togtbl. (55 (59) (63) (67) (71) sts)

Rep above 2 rows 15 times more. (25 (29) (33) (37) (41) sts)

Next row (RS): K2togtbl, cast (bind) off 3 (7) (11) (15) (19) sts, work to end of row as per front left st pattern, removing the st markers. (21 sts)

Cont working on 21 sts as per front left st pattern for 8 (8) (8) (9) (9)cm (3 (3) (3) (3½) (3½)in).

Cut yarn leaving a long enough end to weave in later. Place all 21 sts onto a stitch holder.

72 · Cola Gilet

Front right

Work as Front Left section until end of rib sts.

FR row 1 (RS): K20, PM, p1, k6, PM, k to end.

FR row 2 and all WS rows (WS): P to marker, p6, k1, p to end.

FR row 3: K to marker, p1, C6F, k to end.

FR row 5: K to marker, p1, k6, k to end.

FR row 7: As FR row 5.

FR row 9: K to marker, p1, C6B, k to end.

FR row 11: As FR row 5.

FR row 13: As FR row 5.

The last 12 rows (FR rows 3 to 14) define front right st pattern.

Cont in front right st pattern until work measures 19cm (7½in) from hem, ending on WS row.

PM on last st to mark beg of armhole.

Cont in front right st pattern until work measures 42 (42) (43) (43) (44)cm (16½ (16½) (17) (17) (17¼)in) from hem, ending on a WS row.

Right shoulder shaping

Next row (RS): Work to last 2 sts keeping front right pattern correct, k2tog. (56 (60) (64) (68) (72) sts)

Next row (WS): P2tog, work to end of row keeping front right pattern correct. (55 (59) (63) (67) (71) sts)

Rep the above 2 rows 15 times more. (25 (29) (33) (37) (41) sts)

Next row (RS): Work as per pattern up to last 2 sts, k2tog. (24 (28) (32) (36) (40) sts)

Next row (WS): Cast (bind) off 3 (7) (11) (15) (19) sts, work to end of row as per front right st pattern, removing the st markers. (21 sts)

Cont working on 21 sts following front right st pattern for 8 (8) (8) (9) (9) cm (3 (3) (3) (3½) (3½)in). Do not cast (bind) off.

Assembly and finishing

Join live stitches on both front panel ends using 3-needle cast (see Special Techniques).

Join the back and the front shoulders using joining chain stitch (see Special Techniques) for a decorative-looking join. Alternatively, use mattress stitch (see Special Techniques).

Join back neckline to sides of the front panels using mattress stitch.

Join the side seams from the top of hem rib to beg of arm opening, indicated by st markers, using mattress stitch.

Weave in all ends.

Block for a professional finished look.

The Border Leicester has one of the softest longwool fleeces, which is a natural soft cream colour. As black wool was deliberately bred out of Border Leicesters, I've incorporated Cheviot yarn to produce the contrast cuffs and embroidery. The embroidery design is inspired by the coat of arms of Northumberland, where the breed emerged in the Middle Ages. The scrolling pattern contains shepherd's hooks and sheep bells, creating a unique, cosy sweater.

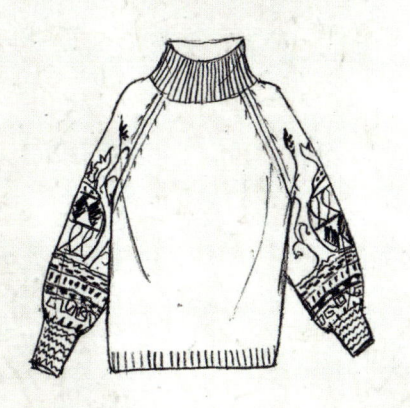

Moina Sweater
in Border Leicester

Pattern Notes

Moina is an oversized and unique sweater that really makes a statement.

This pattern is knitted bottom up, with the body and sleeves worked flat. The sleeves include colourwork sections, which are worked using the stranded knitting technique in the flat where unused strands of yarn are carried across the wrong side of the work. On the mid to upper sleeves, there are hand-embroidered details, as shown on the Embroidery Template.

The pattern is for three sizes: small, medium, and large.

Skill level: for experienced knitters

Materials

YARN

Sheep DK yarn (100% wool), DK, 100g (200m/383yds). Supplied by Doulton Border Leicester

Main colour: Sheep undyed; 500 (500) (600)g; 5 (5) (6) skeins

Machine Spun (100% wool), 4ply, 100g (350m/383yds). Supplied by Heatherlea Black Cheviot

Contrast colour: Shadow undyed; 100g; 1 ball

NEEDLES
- 4mm (US 6)
- 3mm (US 3) circular or DPNs
- Tapestry needle

OTHER
- Stitch markers

Tension (Gauge)

22 sts x 29 rows measures 10cm (4in) square over stocking stitch using 4mm (US 6) needles.

Sizes and Garment Measurements

(Measurements after blocking)

	SMALL	MEDIUM	LARGE
To fit bust	81–86cm (32–34in)	92–97cm (36–38in)	102–107cm (40–42in)
Bust circumference	100cm (39¼in)	110cm (43¼in)	120cm (47¼in)
Length from hem to underarm	35cm (13¾in)	35cm (13¾in)	35cm (13¾in)
Length from hem to upper shoulder	61cm (24in)	62cm (24½in)	63cm (24¾in)
Sleeve length from cuff to underarm	44cm (17¼in)	45cm (17¾in)	46cm (18in)
Upper sleeve circumference	46cm (18in)	48cm (19in)	50cm (19¾in)

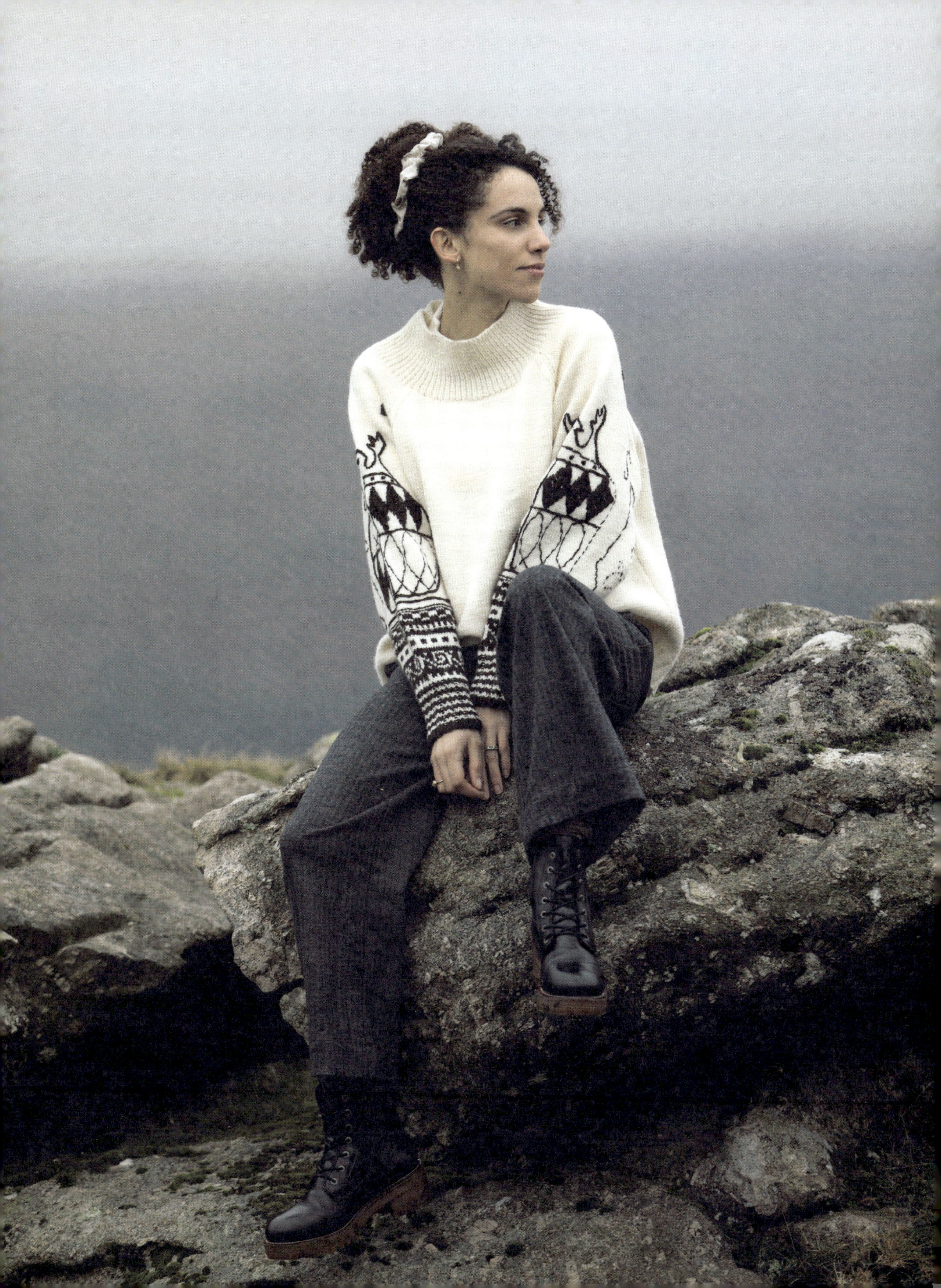

Instructions

Back

Using 4mm (US 6) needles and MC, cast on 110 (122) (134) sts.

Rib row 1 (RS): K2, [p2, k2] to end.

Rib row 2 (WS): P2, [k2, p2] to end.

Rep above 2 rib rows until rib measures 5cm (2in), ending on WS row.

Cont working in ss throughout, starting with k row, until work measures 35 (35) (35)cm (13¾ (13¾) (13¾)in) from cast on edge, ending on WS row.

Back raglan shaping

Cast (bind) off 4 (4) (6) at the start of next 2 rows for underarm. (102 (114) (122) sts)

Starting with knit row, cont in ss for 8 (4) (0) rows.

Using below dec instruction, dec 1 st at each end of next row, then on following 26 (31) (34) alt rows, ending on a WS row:

RS dec row: K2, ssk, k to last 4 sts, k2tog, k2.

48 (50) (52) sts.

Cast (bind) off.

Front

Work as for back until back raglan shaping.

Front raglan shaping

Cast (bind) off 4 (4) (6) at the start of next 2 rows for underarm. (102 (114) (122) sts)

Starting with knit row, cont in ss for 8 (4) (0) rows.

Using below dec instruction, dec 1 st at each end of next row, then on following 22 (27) (30) alt rows, ending on a WS row:

RS dec row: K2, ssk, k to last 4 sts, k2tog, k2.

(56 (58) (60) sts)

Using German short rows (see Special Techniques), shape neckline, at the same time, cont with raglan shaping as follows:

Short row 1 (RS): K2, ssk, k10, turn. (55 (57) (59) sts)

Short row 2 (WS): Wyif sl1p and make DS, p to end.

Short row 3: K2, ssk, k6, turn. (54 (56) (58) sts)

Short row 4: Wyif sl1p and make DS, p to end.

Short row 5: K2, ssk, k3, turn. (53 (55) (57) sts)

Short row 6: Wyif sl1p and make DS, p to end.

Row 7: K2, ssk, k to last 4 sts making sure each DS is worked as 1 st, k2tog, k2. (51 (53) (55) sts)

Short row 8: P13, turn.

Short row 9: Wyif sl1p and make DS, k to last 4 sts, k2tog, k2. (50 (52) (54) sts)

Short row 10: P9, turn.

Short row 11: Wyif sl1p and make DS, k to last 4 sts, k2tog, k2. (49 (51) (53) sts)

Short row 12: P6, turn.

Short row 13: Wyif sl1p and make DS, k to last 4 sts, k2tog, k2. (48 (50) (52) sts)

Short row 14: P to end.

Cast (bind) off.

Sleeves (make 2)

CC yarn is worked with 2 strands held together throughout the cuff and colourwork sections.

Using 4mm (US 6) needles and CC, held double by working with 2 ends of the wool/yarn, cast on 54 sts.

Rib row 1 (RS): K2, [p2, k2] to end.

Rib row 2 (WS): P2, [k2, p2] to end.

Change to MC.

Rep rib rows 1 and 2.

Change to CC.

Rep rib rows 1 and 2.

Rep the last 4 rows 4 times more.

Change to MC.

Rep rib rows 1 and 2 once again.

Colourwork section

Start colourwork section following Chart A (rows 1-32), at the same time, using inc instructions below, inc 1 st at each end of 3rd row and on subsequent alt rows until all rows in Chart A are worked:

Inc row for all RS row except row 23: Work 1 st as per chart, M1L, work to last st as per chart, M1R, work 1 st as per chart.

Inc row 23 (RS): With MC, p1, M1LP, p to last st, M1RP, p1.

84 sts.

With MC, working in ss throughout, continue inc 1 st at each end of next row and subsequent 1 (3) (3) alt rows, followed by 0 (0) (9) 6th rows, followed by 7 (7) (0) 8th rows, using same inc instruction as above.

102 (106) (110) sts.

Continue working straight until work measures 44 (45) (46)cm (17¼ (17¾) (18)in).

Cast (bind) off 4 (4) (6) at the start of next 2 rows for underarm. (94 (98) (98) sts)

Sleeve raglan shaping

Work in ss for (2) (2) (4) rows.

Using below dec instruction, dec 1 st at each end of next row, then on the following 29 (31) (31) alt rows, ending on a WS row:

RS dec row: K2, ssk, k to last 4 sts, k2tog, k2.

34 (34) (34) sts.

Number of rows worked from underarm cast (bind) off to the top of raglan shaping should be 62 (66) (68).

Cast (bind) off.

Embroidery

With one strand of CC, embroider the sleeves above the colourwork area following the Embroidery Template as a guide. The sample modelled in the photo is made using a combination of embroidery stitches:

1) Chain stitch is indicated on the template by smooth lines.

2) Back stitch is indicated by dashed lines.

3) Long-and-short stitches are indicated by shaded areas.

4) Lazy daisy stitch is used for the 2 flowers.

To make the shaded areas neat, back stitch is used to create an outline around the long-and-short stitching.

The template is shown at full size and can be traced or photocopied. A printable version is available from www.bookmarkedhub.com.

Please refer to the schematic for how the pieces should be joined together.

Assembly and finishing

Join the front and back to the sleeves along the raglan sides using mattress stitch in the ditch between the edge sts and the next sts of each piece. The ditch is the area between 2 adjacent stitches.

Join the side seams of the front and back and the underarm seams using mattress stitch.

Neck

Using 3mm (US 3) circular or DPNs, starting from the back left raglan point, pick up and knit 34 sts along the top of the left sleeve neck edge, then pick up and knit 46 (48) (50) sts along the front edge, pick up and knit 34 sts along the top of the right sleeve neck edge, then pick up and knit 46 (48) (50) sts along the back neck edge. Place marker to indicate BOR/EOR. (160 (164) (168) sts)

Work in 1x1 rib in the rnd for 42 rounds as follows:

[K1, p1] to EOR.

Cast (bind) off.

Weave in ends.

Block for a professional finished look.

Moina Sweater • 79

EMBROIDERY TEMPLATE

KEY

— Chain stitch

- - - Back stitch

▬ Long and short stitch

✿ Lacy Daisy Stitch

A

80 · Moina Sweater

Moina Sweater • 81

C

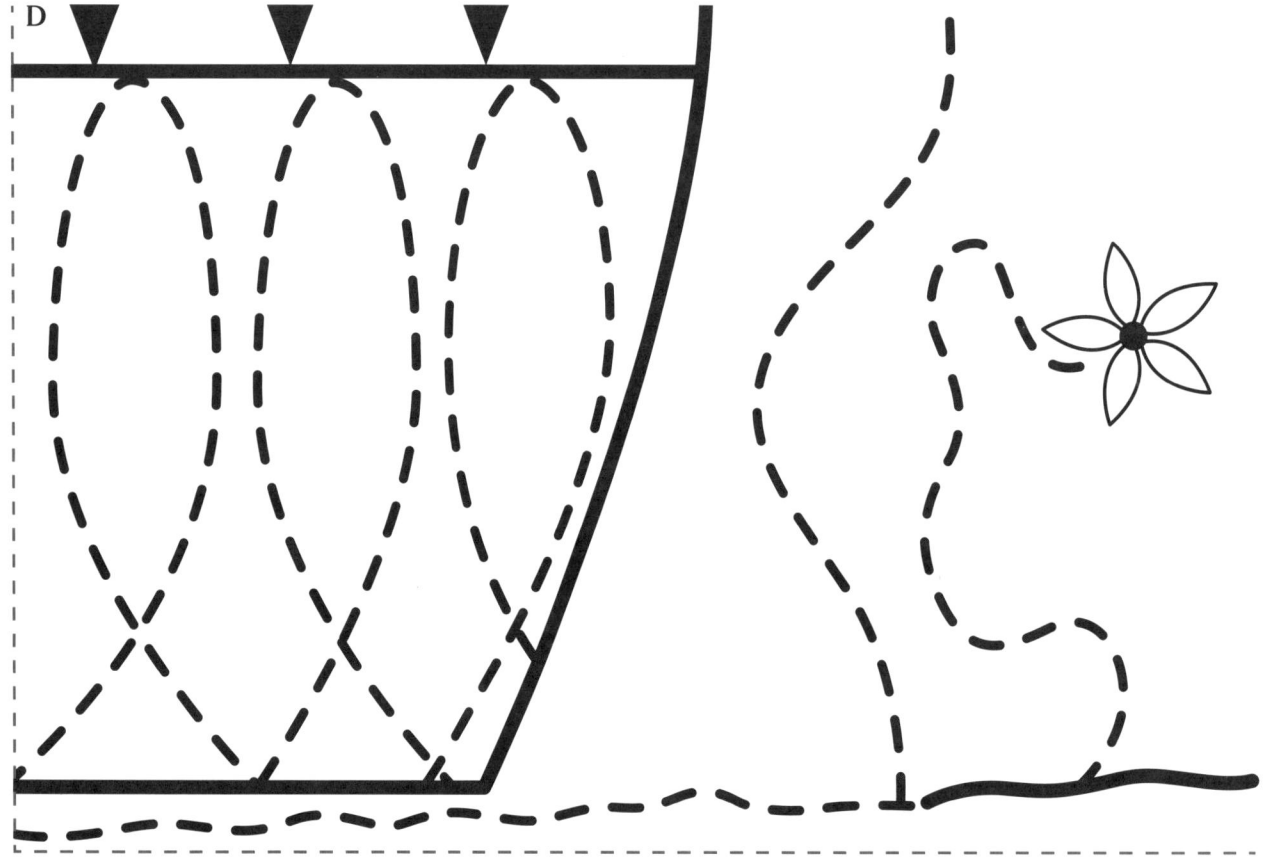

D

82 · Moina Sweater

CHART A: COLOURWORK SECTION

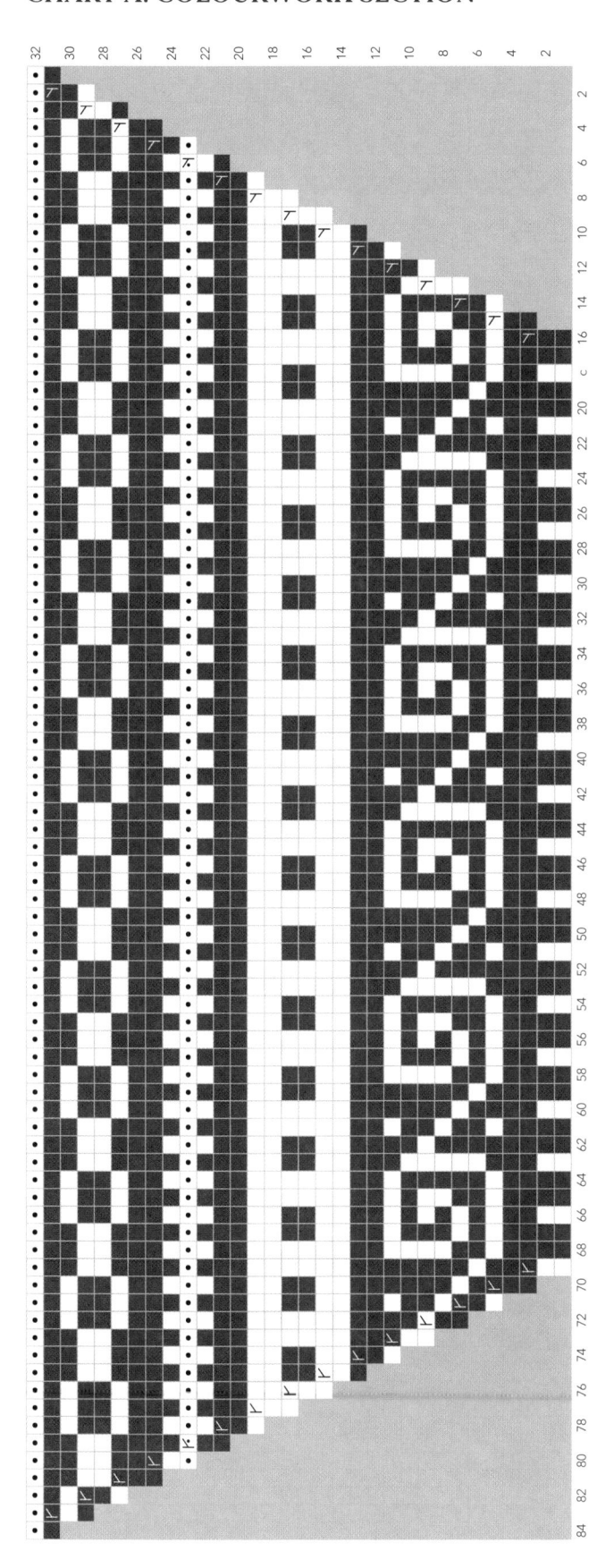

KEY

□	RS: knit / WS: purl
•	RS: knit / WS: purl
□ (white)	MC: Sheep Undyed
■ (black)	CC: Shadow Undyed
▢ (grey)	no stitch
ʏ	RS: M1R – right-leaning increase
ʏ	RS: M1L – left-leaning increase
ʏ	RS: M1 purlwise left leaning
ʏ	RS: M1 purlwise right leaning

Chart Note

Chart A gives a visual representation of the colourwork section of the pattern.

The starting point of Chart A is the bottom right. Odd-number rows are RS rows and are read from right to left. Even-number rows are WS rows and are read from left to right.

Each square represents one stitch. The colour of the square indicates the shade of yarn to be used for that action. A symbol inside the square indicates what stitch. If the square is blank, with no symbol, then the instruction is to knit when on RS and purl when on WS. The symbols and their meaning are listed in the key.

Moina Sweater • 83

The Bluefaced Leicester (known as the BFL) has the softest handle of all the longwools. This, along with its beautiful and luxurious lustre, makes it a very popular yarn. I created a Fair Isle design in order to showcase the natural colours: soft, creamy brown, ecru and dark brown. To enhance the beauty of the sweater, I've used a roving yarn – produced with minimal twist for extra softness.

Carril Fair Isle Jumper
in Bluefaced Leicester

Pattern Notes

Carril is a cosy jumper in the Fair Isle tradition. It has yoke-style construction and is worked on circular needles from the top down. The knit grows quickly due to the larger 5mm (US 8) needle size.

Using German short rows (see Special Techniques) at the base of the neckline ensures a comfortable fit. The stranded knitting technique is used throughout – unused strands of yarn are carried across the wrong side of the work.

Above the rib, there's a single stitch cable that creates extra interest at the hem and cuffs.

The pattern is written for five sizes: Small, medium, large, X-large, and XX-large.

Skill level: for experienced knitters

Materials

YARN

Fleece Bluefaced Leicester Aran (100% wool), aran, 100g (150m/164yds). Supplied by West Yorkshire Spinners

Main colour: Light Brown 002; 600 (700) (700) (800) (900)g; 6 (7) (7) (8) (9) skeins

Contrast colour 1: Ecru 001; 200 (200) (300) (300) (300)g; 2 (2) (3) (3) (3) skeins

Contrast colour 2: Brown 003; 100g; 1 skein

NEEDLES
- 5mm (US 8) circular needles
- 5mm (US 8) DPNs for the sleeves
- Cable needle

OTHER
- Stitch markers
- 2 stitch holders or stitch wires to hold sleeve stitches

Tension (Gauge)

19 sts x 22 rows measures 10cm (4in) square over stranded stocking stitch using 5mm (US 8) circular needles. Be sure to swatch with DPNs or sleeve-size circular needles as well, as your tension in smaller circular knitting might differ from your larger circular knitting. Adjust if needed.

Sizes and Garment Measurements

(Measurements after blocking)

	SMALL	MEDIUM	LARGE	X-LARGE	XX-LARGE
To fit bust	81-86cm (32-34in)	92-97cm (36-38in)	102-107cm (40-42in)	112-117cm (44-46in)	122-127cm (48-50in)
Bust circumference	110cm (43¼in)	118.5cm (46½in)	127cm (50in)	135.5cm (53¼in)	143cm (56¼in)
Length from hem to underarm	36cm (14in)	36cm (14in)	37cm (14½in)	38cm (15in)	38cm (15in)
Length from hem to upper shoulder	63cm (24¾in)	64cm (25in)	65cm (25½in)	66cm (26in)	66cm (26in)
Sleeve length from cuff to underarm	41cm (16in)	42cm (16½in)	43cm (17in)	44cm (17¼in)	44cm (17¼in)
Upper sleeve circumference	34cm (13¼in)	35cm (13¾in)	36cm (14in)	37cm (14½in)	38cm (15in)

86 · Carril Fair Isle Jumper

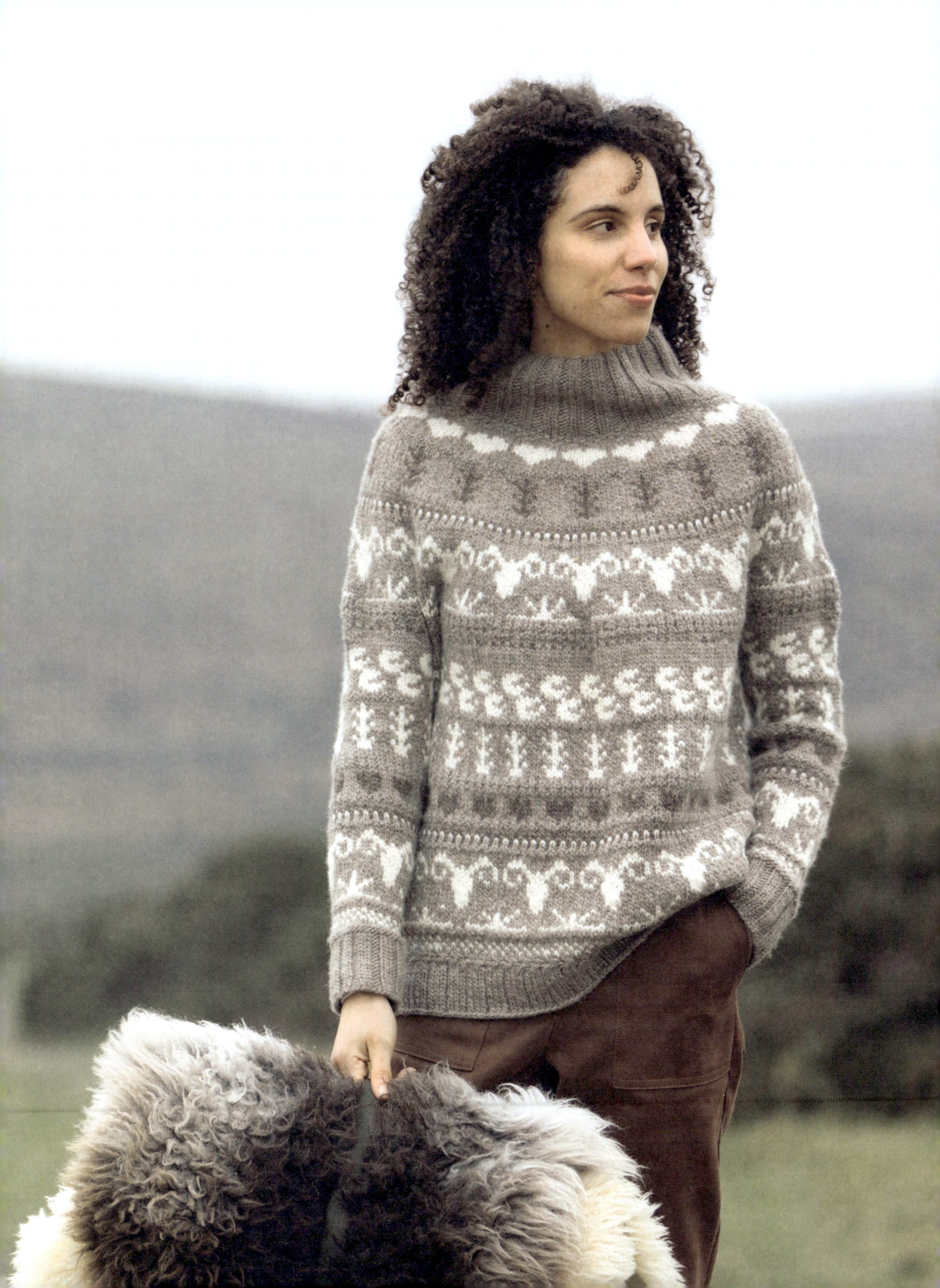

Instructions

Neck

Using MC, cast on 96 (100) (104) (108) (108) sts. Join ends to work in the rnd making sure work is not twisted. PM on the needle to indicate EOR/BOR.

Note: BOR/EOR is in the centre of back. Always SM when encountering it.

Rib rnd (RS): [K2, p2] to EOR.

Rep rib rnd until work measures 11cm (4¼in).

Neck short-row shaping

Continue working in rib for the neck short row shaping. Use German short rows (see Special Techniques) or a preferred alternative short-row technique.

Short row 1 (RS): Work 23 (24) (25) (26) (26) sts in rib as above. Turn.

Short row 2 (WS): Work in rib to EOR. Continue in rib for 23 (24) (25) (26) (26) sts. Turn.

Short row 3: Work in rib to EOR. Cont in rib up to 4 sts before turn in short row 1. Turn.

Short row 4: Work in rib to EOR. Cont in rib up to 4 sts before turn in short row 2. Turn.

Short row 5: Work in rib to EOR. Cont in rib up to 4 sts before turn in short row 3. Turn.

Short row 6: Work in rib to EOR. Cont in rib up to 4 sts before turn in short row 4. Turn.

Row 7 (RS): Work to EOR.

Yoke

FOR SIZE M ONLY:

Inc by 2 sts.

Inc rnd: K -- (25) (--) (--) (--), M1L, k -- (50) (--) (--) (--), M1L, k to EOR.

FOR SIZE L ONLY:

Inc by 4 sts.

Inc rnd: *K -- (--) (25) (--) (--), M1L, rep from * 3 times more, k to EOR.

FOR SIZE XL ONLY:

Inc by 6 sts.

Inc rnd: *K -- (--) (--) (17) (--), M1L, rep from * 5 times more, k to EOR.

FOR SIZE XXL ONLY:

Inc by 12 sts.

Inc rnd: *K -- (--) (--) (--) (8), M1L, rep from * 11 times more, k to EOR.

(96 (102) (108) (114) (120) sts)

Next, work yoke colourwork section following Chart A.

There are 16 (17) (18) (19) (20) yoke pattern repeats.

At end of chart, there are 288 (306) (324) (342) (360) sts.

Cut CC1 and CC2, leaving enough tail length to weave in end. Continue with MC.

FOR SIZES SM, L, XL ONLY:

Inc rnd: *K24 (--) (81) (57) (--), M1L, rep from * to EOR.

FOR SIZE M ONLY:

Inc rnd: *K30, M1L, rep from * to last 6 sts, k6.

FOR SIZE XXL ONLY:

No increase. K to EOR.

FOR ALL SIZES:

There are 300 (316) (328) (348) (360) sts.

Separate body from sleeves

Next rnd: Using MC, starting from BOR k47 (51) (54) (58) (61) for one half of back, place the next 56 (56) (56) (58) (58) sts for right sleeve on a st holder or st wire.

Cast on 10 (10) (12) (12) (14) sts for right underarm, k94 (102) (108) (116) (122) for front body, place next 56 (56) (56) (58) (58) sts for left sleeve on a st holder or st wire.

Cast on 10 (10) (12) (12) (14) sts for left underarm, k47 (51) (54) (58) (61) for other half of back. (208 (224) (240) (256) (272) sts)

Body

Work 1 (3) (3) (3) (3) rnds of ss.

Work body colourwork section following Chart B.

There are 13 (14) (15) (16) (17) body pattern repeats.

Cut CC1 and CC2 leaving enough tail length to weave in end.

With MC work 0 (0) (2) (4) (4) rnds of ss.

Body hem

Hem rnd 1: Using MC, [C3B, p1] to EOR.

Hem rnd 2: [K3, p1] to EOR.

Hem rnd 3: [C3F, p1] to EOR.

Rnds 4-11: As Hem rnd 2.

Cast (bind) off in pattern.

Sleeves (make 2)

Transfer the sts of one sleeve onto the main needle.

Join MC yarn at the centre of the underarm of the body with RS facing up, pick up and knit 5 (5) (6) (6) (7) sts until the sleeve sts are met. Knit the sleeve sts. Then pick up and knit 5 (5) (6) (6) (7) sts to complete rnd. PM to mark the BOR/EOR in the centre of armpit. (66 (66) (68) (70) (72) sts)

Work 0 (2) (2) (2) (2) rnds of ss.

Work sleeve colourwork section following Chart C, paying attention to shaping by dec 1 st at both ends of the 6th rnd and every subsequent 6th rnd 11 (11, 12, 11, 12) times, as follows:

K1, SSK, work as per chart, keeping pattern correct until 3 sts before EOR, k2tog, k1. When chart is finished, before decreases are complete, continue in MC working in ss until target st counts are achieved.

(44 (44) (44) (48) (48) sts)

With MC, cont in ss until sleeve measures 32 (33) (34) (35) (35)cm (12½ (13) (13¼) (13¾) (13¾)in).

Work 2 rnds in reverse ss (i.e. 2 rnds of purl).

Cuff rib

Cuff rnd 1: Using MC, [k2, p2] to EOR.

Rep cuff rnd until cuff rib measures 8cm (3in).

Cast (bind) off in pattern.

Finishing

Cast (bind) off in pattern.

Weave in all ends.

Block for a professional finished look.

Carril Fair Isle Jumper • 89

CHART A – YOKE

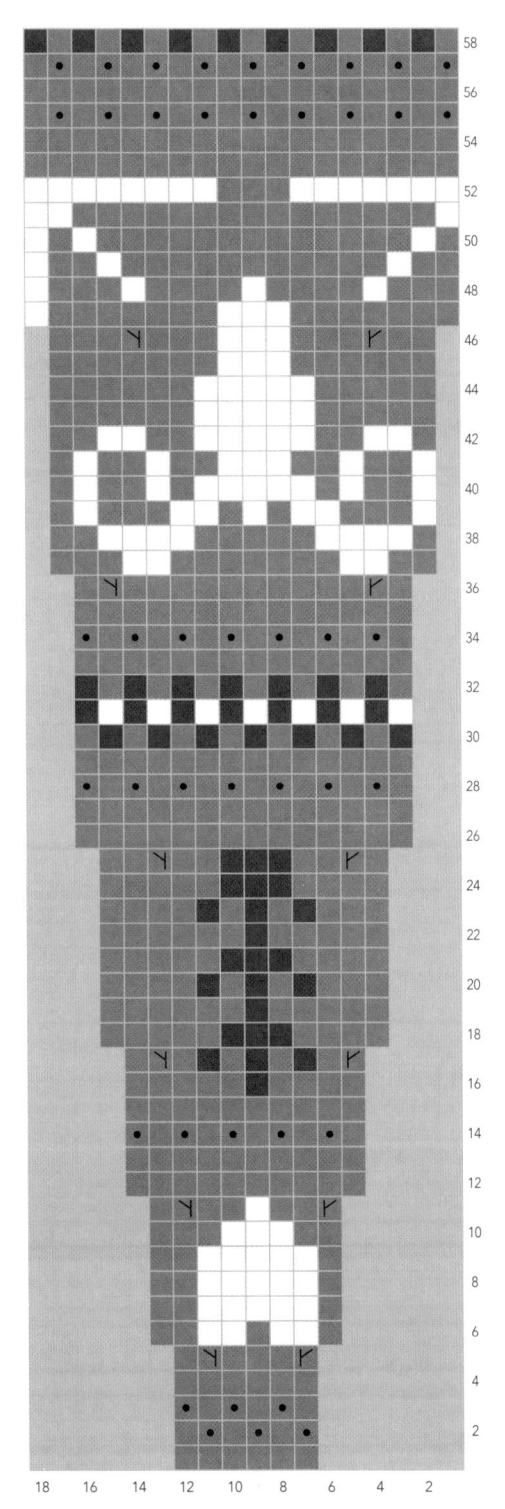

KEY

- MC – Light brown 002
- CC1 – Ecru 001
- CC2 – Brown 003
- • Purl
- Knit
- M1L – left-leaning increase
- M1R – right-leaning increase
- No stitch

Chart Note

Each square represents one stitch. The colour of the square indicates the shade of yarn to be used. A symbol inside the square indicates what action to work.

CHART B – BODY

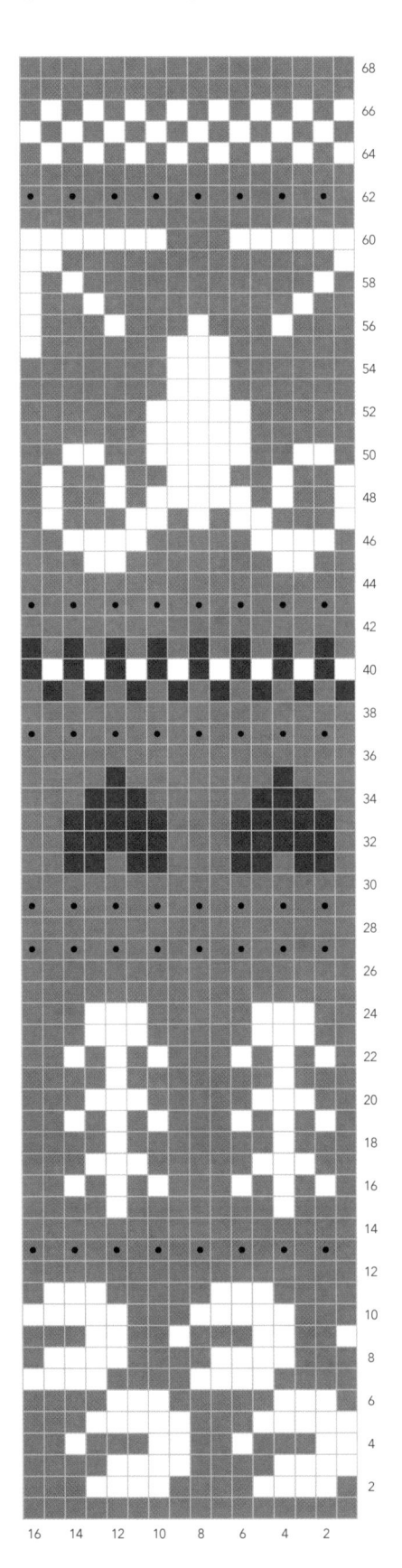

90 • Carril Fair Isle Jumper

CHART C - SLEEVE

CHART C SIZE KEY

- XXL
- XL
- L
- S and M

Carril Fair Isle Jumper • 91

The pretty Castlemilk Moorit produces a soft reddish-brown fleece that needs to be sorted carefully, otherwise it can be quite rough. In this project, it's combined with Bluefaced Leicester to create extra softness and enhance cable patterns. This covetable cardigan is suitable for both everyday and smarter wear. It's knitted in its natural nutmeg colour and named after the Celtic Tara Hills.

Tara Cardigan
in Castlemilk Moorit

Pattern Notes

The Tara cardigan is a pleasingly oversized style with dropped shoulders.

The pattern is knitted bottom up with the body and sleeves worked flat. The front body features a ribbed cable, with the cable repeating every 10th row, which makes this a quick knit.

The cuffs and hem have an alternating rib and cable pattern. The rest of the body is knitted in plain stocking stitch. The front trim includes a central cable and is knitted integrally, which saves on making-up time.

As this garment is very oversized, the pattern is written in two sizes only: small/medium and large/X-large.

Skill level: for intermediate to experienced knitters

Materials

YARN
Castlemilk Moorit / Bluefaced Leicester blend (100% wool), 4-ply, 100g (380m/415yds). Supplied by Dodgson Wood

Shade: Natural brown; 550 (650)g; 6 (7) skeins with 2 strands held together throughout

NEEDLES
- 4.5mm (US 7) needles
- Cable needle

OTHER
- Darning needle
- 4 stitch markers
- 3 x 2.5cm (1in) buttons. It's quite effective to use three different styles of button, but they should be of similar sizes to fit through the buttonholes.

Tension (Gauge)

18 sts x 29 rows measures 10cm (4in) square over stocking stitch using 4.5mm (US 7) needles.

Sizes and Garment Measurements

(Measurements after blocking)

	SMALL/MEDIUM	LARGE/X-LARGE
To fit bust	81-97cm (32-38in)	102-117cm (40-46in)
Bust circumference	120cm (47¼in)	130cm (51¼in)
Length back hem to upper shoulder	50cm (19¾in)	52cm (20½in)
Length back hem to lower shoulder	47cm (18½in)	49cm (19¼in)
Length front hem to lower shoulder	44cm (17¼in)	46cm (18in)
Sleeve length from underarm to cuff	44.5cm (17½in)	46.5cm (18¼in)
Upper sleeve circumference	41cm (16in)	44cm (17¼in)

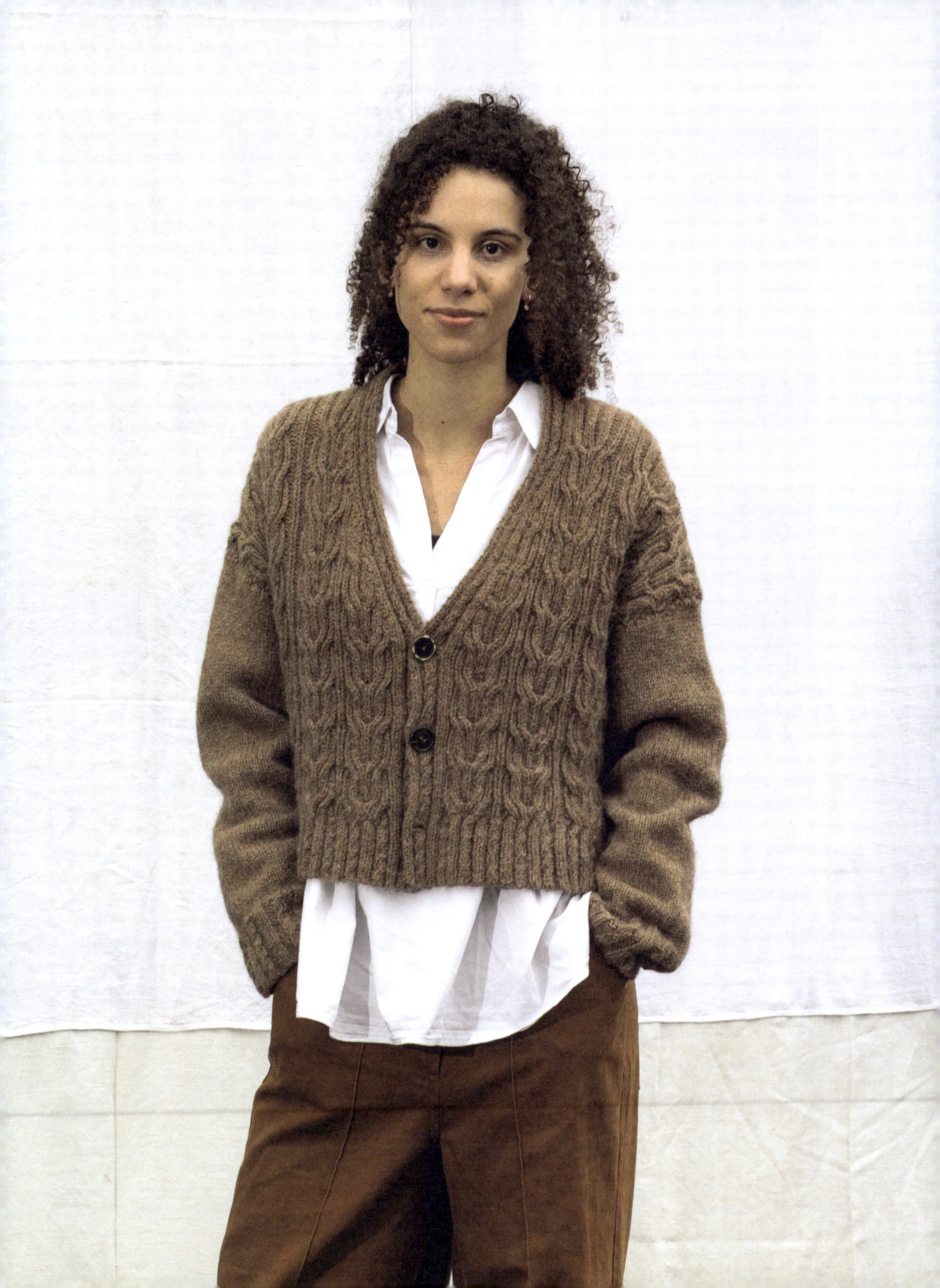

Instructions

Back

Using 2 strands of yarn held together throughout, cast on 130 (142) sts.

FOR SIZE S/M ONLY:

Rib row 1 (RS): K2, [p2, k2] to end.

Rib row 2 (WS): P2, [k2, p2] to end.

Rib row 3: K2, [p2, RT, p2, k2] to end.

Rib row 4: As Rib row 2.

Rep Rib rows 1-4 six times more, dec by 22 sts on last rib row as follows:

Rib row 28 (WS): P2, *[k2tog, p2] twice, k2, p2; rep from * to last 8 sts, [k2tog, p2] twice. (108 (-) sts)

FOR SIZE L/XL ONLY:

Rib row 1 (RS): P2, [k2, p2] to end.

Rib row 2 (WS): K2, [p2, k2] to end.

Rib row 3: P2, [RT, p2, k2, p2] to last 4 sts, RT, p2.

Rib row 4: As Rib row 2.

Rep rib rows 1 to 4 six more times, dec by 24 sts on last rib row as follows:

Rib row 28 (WS): *[K2tog, p2] twice, k2, p2; rep from * to last 10 sts, [k2tog, p2] twice, k2. (- (118) sts)

FOR BOTH SIZES:

Next row (RS): k to end.

Next row (WS): P to end.

Above 2 rows define ss pattern. Cont working in ss until work measures 47 (49)cm (18½ (19¼)in) from cast on edge, ending on a WS row.

Shape shoulders and back neckline

Cast (bind) off 8 (9) sts at beg of next 2 rows working rest of row in ss. (92 (100) sts)

Cast (bind) off 8 (9) sts at beg of next 2 rows working rest of row in ss. (76 (82) sts)

Cast (bind) off 8 (9) sts at beg of next 2 rows working rest of row in ss. (60 (64) sts)

Cast (bind) off 8 (9) sts at beg of next 2 rows working rest of row in ss. (44 (46) sts)

Cast (bind) off 8 sts at beg of next 2 rows working rest of row in ss. (28 (30) sts)

Cast (bind) off rem sts representing back neckline.

Front right

Front pieces are worked with frontband along with front body. With RS of work facing you, the first 10 sts make up frontband of Front Right. Follow Chart A for frontband pattern.

Using 2 strands of yarn held together throughout, cast on 84 (88) sts.

FR rib row 1 (RS): K2, [p2, k2] twice, PM, [p2, k2] to last 2 sts, p2.

Note: Stitch marker is a delimiter separating frontband from rest of Front Right sts. Front band is a 4-rows rep pattern worked throughout Front Right.

FR rib rows 2 and 4 (WS): K2, [p2, k2] to marker, SM, [p2, k2] twice, p2.

FR rib row 3: K2, p2, RT, p2, k2, SM, [p2, k2] to last 2 (6) sts, p2.

FR rib rows 1 to 4 define Front Right rib st pattern. Rep these 4 rows twice more.

FR rib row 13: K2, p1, make a 4-st buttonhole (see Special Techniques), p1, k2, SM, [p2, k2] to last 2 sts, p2.

FR rib rows 14 and 15: As FR rib row 2 and 3.

Increase on next and final FR rib row by 3 (4) sts as follows:

FOR SIZE S/M ONLY:

FR rib row 16 (WS): K2, [p2, k2] 4 times, M1L [p2, k2] 5 times, M1L, [p2, k2] 5 times, M1L, [p2, k2] 4 times, SM, [p2, k2] twice, p2. (87 (-) sts)

FOR SIZE L/XL ONLY:

FR rib row 16 (WS): K2, p2, M1L, k2, [p2, k2] 4 times, M1L, [p2, k2] 5 times, M1L, [p2, k2] 5 times, M1L, [p2, k2] 4 times, SM, [p2, k2] twice, p2. (- (92) sts)

For rows 17 onwards, follow Chart B.

Row 17 (RS): Frontband pattern, SM, *p1, k1, [p2, k2] 3 times, p2, k1, p1, k1; rep from * 3 more times, p1, k0 (1), p0 (2), k0 (1), p0 (1).

Row 18 (WS): K0 (1), p0 (1), k0 (2), p0 (1), k1, *p1, k1, p1, k2, [p2, k2] 3 times, p1, k1; rep from * 3 times more, SM, frontband pattern.

Row 19: Frontband pattern, SM, *p1, RCB, RCF, p1, k1; rep from * 3 times more, p1, k0 (1), p0 (2), K0 (1), p0 (1).

Row 20: As row 18.

Row 21: As row 17.

Row 22: As row 18.

Row 23: As row 17.

Row 24: As row 18.

Rows 17 to 24 define Front Right st pattern.

Continue in this pattern until work measures 12 (13)cm (4¾ (5)in), ending on WS of work.

Next row (RS): K2, p1, make a 4-st buttonhole (see Special Techniques), p1, k2, SM, work rem sts keeping pattern correct.

Continue in Front Right st pattern until work measures 20 (22)cm (7¾ (8¾)in), ending on WS of work.

Next row (RS): K2, p1, make a 4-st buttonhole (see Special Techniques), p1, k2, SM, work rem sts keeping pattern correct.

Continue in Front Right st pattern until work measures 21 (23)cm (8¼ (9)in), ending on WS of work.

Shape neckline and shoulder

Decrease 1 st at neck edge on next and every following 27 (28) alt rows, as follows:

Work first 9 sts of frontband (up to 1 st before marker), RM, ssk, PM, work rem sts keeping pattern correct.

Note: Marker is in between 2 sts to be decreased. Remove it before decrease and reposition it after decrease.

Continue straight until work measures 44 (46)cm (17¼ (18)in), ending on RS of work.

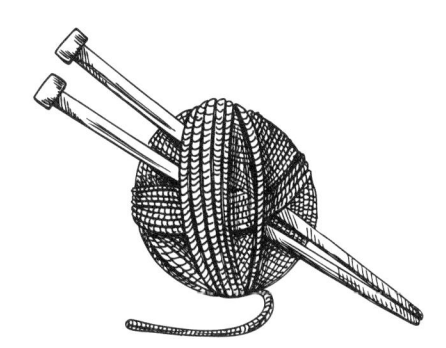

Start shaping shoulders as follows:

Next row (WS): Cast (bind) off 10 (11) sts in pattern, work rem sts as per pattern.

Work 1 row as per pattern.

Rep last 2 rows three times more.

Cast (bind) off 9 sts in pattern, work rem sts as per pattern. (10 sts)

Continue working rem frontband sts for 20 more rows.

Cast (bind) off in pattern.

Front left

Front pieces are worked with frontband along with front body. With RS of work facing you, the last 10 sts make up frontband of Front Left. Follow Chart A for frontband pattern.

Cast on 84 (88) sts.

FL rib row 1 (RS): [P2, k2] to last 12 sts, p2, PM, k2, [p2, k2] twice.

Note: Stitch marker is a delimiter separating frontband (i.e. last 10 sts when facing RS of work) from rest of front left sts. Frontband is a 4 rows rep pattern worked throughout front left.

FL rib row 2 and 4 (WS): [P2, k2] twice, p2, SM, [k2, p2] to last 2 sts, k2.

FOR SIZE S/M ONLY:

FL rib row 3: [P2, k2, p2, RT] to 2 sts before marker, p2, SM, k2, p2, RT, p2, k2.

FOR SIZE L/XL ONLY:

FL rib row 3: [P2, RT, p2, k2] to 6 sts before marker, p2, RT, p2, SM, k2, p2, RT, p2, k2.

BOTH SIZES:

FL rib rows 1 to 4 define Front Left rib st pattern. Rep these 4 rows three times more, increasing on final FL rib row by 3 (4) sts as follows:

FOR SIZE S/M ONLY:

FL rib row 16 (WS): [P2, k2] twice, p2, SM, [k2, p2] 4 times, M1L [k2, p2] 5 times, M1L, [k2, p2] 5 times, M1L, [k2, p2] 4 times, k2. (87 (-) sts)

FOR SIZE L/XL ONLY:

FL rib row 16 (WS): [P2, k2] twice, p2, SM, [k2, p2] 4 times, M1L, [k2, p2] 5 times, M1L, [k2, p2] 5 times, M1L, [k2, p2] 4 times, k2, M1L, p2, k2. (- (92) sts)

For rows 17 onwards, follow Chart C.

Row 17 (RS): P0 (1), k0 (1), p0 (2), k0 (1), p1, *k1, p1, k1, [p2, k2] 3 times, p2, k1, p1; rep from * 3 times more, SM, frontband pattern.

Row 18 (WS): Frontband pattern, SM, *k1, p1, [k2, p2] 3 times, k2, p1, k1, p1; rep from * 3 times more, k1, p0 (1), k0 (2), p0 (1), k0 (1).

Row 19: P0 (1), k0 (1), p0 (2), k0 (1), p1, *k1, p1, RCB, RCF, p1; rep from * 3 times more, SM, frontband pattern.

Row 20: As row 18.

Row 21: As row 17.

Row 22: As row 18.

Row 23: As row 17.

Row 24: As row 18.

Rows 17 to 24 define front left st pattern. Continue in this pattern until work measures 21 (23)cm (8¼ (9)in) ending on WS of work.

Shape neckline and shoulders

Decrease 1 st at neck edge on next and every following 27 (28) alt rows, as follows:

Work as per pattern to 1 st before marker, RM, reposition marker 1 st to right by placing on right needle, k2tog, work rem sts keeping frontband pattern correct.

Continue straight until work measures 44 (46)cm (17¼ (18)in), ending on WS.

Start shaping shoulders as follows:

Next row (RS): Cast (bind) off 10 (11) sts in pattern, work rem sts as per pattern.

Work 1 row as per pattern.

Rep last 2 rows three times more.

Cast (bind) off 9 sts in pattern, work rem sts as per pattern. (10 sts)

Continue working rem front band sts for 20 more rows.

Cast (bind) off in pattern.

Sleeves (make 2)

Cast on 49 (53) sts using 2 strands of yarn held together throughout.

Sleeve rib row 1 (RS): [K2, p2] to last st, k1.

Sleeve rib row 2 and 4 (WS): P1, [k2, p2] to end.

Sleeve rib row 3: [K2, p2, RT, p2] to last 1 (5) sts, k1 (2), p0 (2), k0 (k1).

Above 4 rows define sleeve rib pattern, rep these 4 rows four times more. There should be 20 rows of rib.

Beg working in ss, AT THE SAME TIME, inc 1 st at each end of next and every 6th row five times, followed by every 6th (8th) row until the number of sts on the needle is 75 (79) sts. Inc rows are worked as follows: K1, M1L, k to last st, M1R, k1.

Cont in ss straight until sleeve measures 44 (46)cm (17¼ (18)in) or desired length ending on a WS row.

Next, shape sleeve cap as follows:

Cast (bind) off 6 (7) sts at beg of next 2 rows working rest of row in ss. (63 (65) sts)

Cast (bind) off 6 sts at beg of next 2 rows working rest of row in ss. (51 (53) sts)

Cast (bind) off 6 sts at beg of next 2 rows working rest of row in ss. (39 (41) sts)

Cast (bind) off 6 sts at beg of next 2 rows working rest of row in ss. (27 (29) sts)

Cast (bind) off 6 sts at beg of next 2 rows working rest of row in ss. (15 (17) sts)

Cast (bind) off rem sts.

Assembly and finishing

For best results, use mattress stitch to join all seams.

Join cast (bound) off edge of neckband front right to cast (bound) off edge of neckband front left.

Join front to back along shoulder seam and neckband (i.e. neckband from front pieces to neckbase of back.)

Note: there are more cast (bound) off sts on the front shoulder than the back, so ease extra length of front pieces when sewing shoulder seam.

Place 4 markers 21 (22)cm (8¼ (8¾)in) away on either side of shoulder seam along edge of body to indicate where sleeves are to be joined.

Join cast (bound) off edges of sleeves to body along armholes using markers on body as a guide for the start and end points for seaming.

Join underarm.

Join side seam. Note that the sides of the back are 3cm (1¼in) longer by design.

Sew on 3 buttons.

Weave in ends.

Block for a professional finished look.

CHART A: FRONTBAND

CHART B: FRONT RIGHT

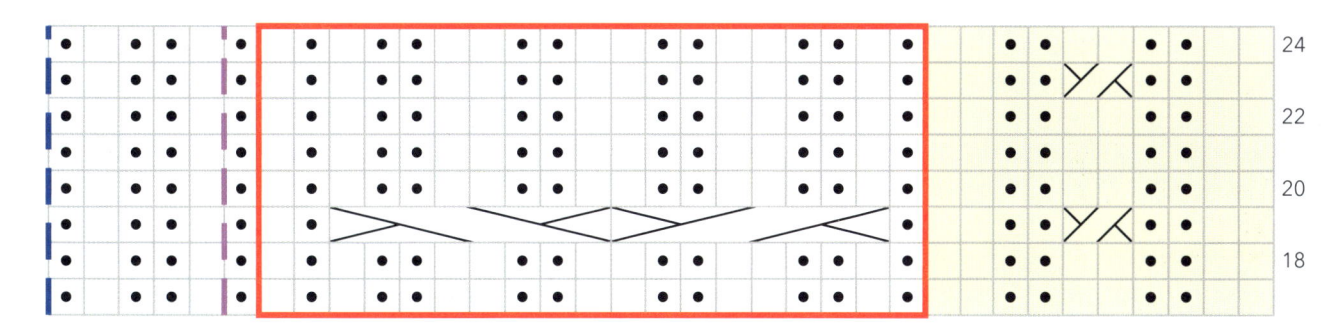

CHART C: FRONT LEFT

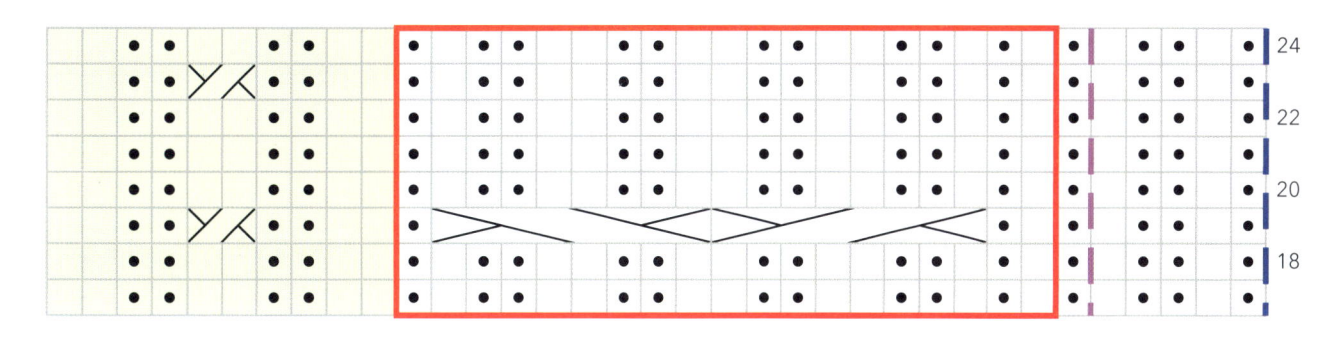

CHART KEY

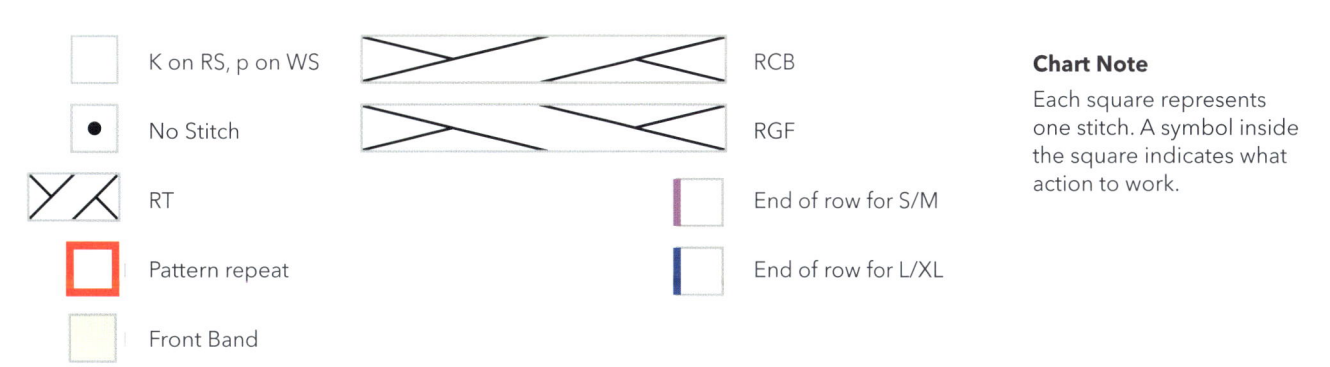

	K on RS, p on WS
•	No Stitch
⋊⋉	RT
▭	Pattern repeat
	Front Band

⋈	RCB
⋈	RGF
▯	End of row for S/M
▮	End of row for L/XL

Chart Note

Each square represents one stitch. A symbol inside the square indicates what action to work.

Tara Cardigan • 99

Jacob sheep are uniquely multi-coloured, incorporating soft white, grey and dark brown in their fleeces. This may not be the softest yarn but it's perfect for accessories. Handspun yarn makes all the difference to this hat design, as the twist of natural colours adds a textured, tweed effect.

Atha Checkered Hat
in Jacob

Pattern Notes

The Atha is a cosy, Nordic-style knitted hat. Stranded knitting is used throughout, meaning the unused strands of yarn are carried across the wrong side of the work.

The hat is knitted with circular needles, which saves time at the making-up stage. If you find it becomes harder to knit as the stitches decrease, switch to double-ended cable needles (see image below).

The trim is knitted with an alternating rib and cable pattern.

This pattern is one size only.

Skill level: for intermediate knitters

Materials

YARN

Fleece Jacob Aran Yarn (100% wool), aran, 100g (166m/182yds). Supplied by West Yorkshire Spinners

Main colour: Medium Grey (006); 50g; 1 skein

Contrast colour 1: Ecru (001); 25g; 1 skein

Contrast colour 2: Brown Black (007); 25g, 1skein

Hand Spun Jacob Yarn (100% wool), 50g. Supplied by The Lost Sheep Company

Contrast colour 3: Marl; 25g; 1 skein

NEEDLES

- 3.5mm (US 4)
- 4.5mm (US 7) 40cm (16in) circular needles or DPNs, or needle size that will yield specified tension (gauge)
- Cable needle
- Tapestry needle

OTHER

- 1 stitch marker

Tension (Gauge)

19 sts x 26 rows measures 10cm (4in) square over stranded knitting using 4.5mm (US 7) needles.

Garment Measurements

(Measurements after blocking)

Head circumference: 49cm (19¼in)

Depth of hat: 18cm (7in)

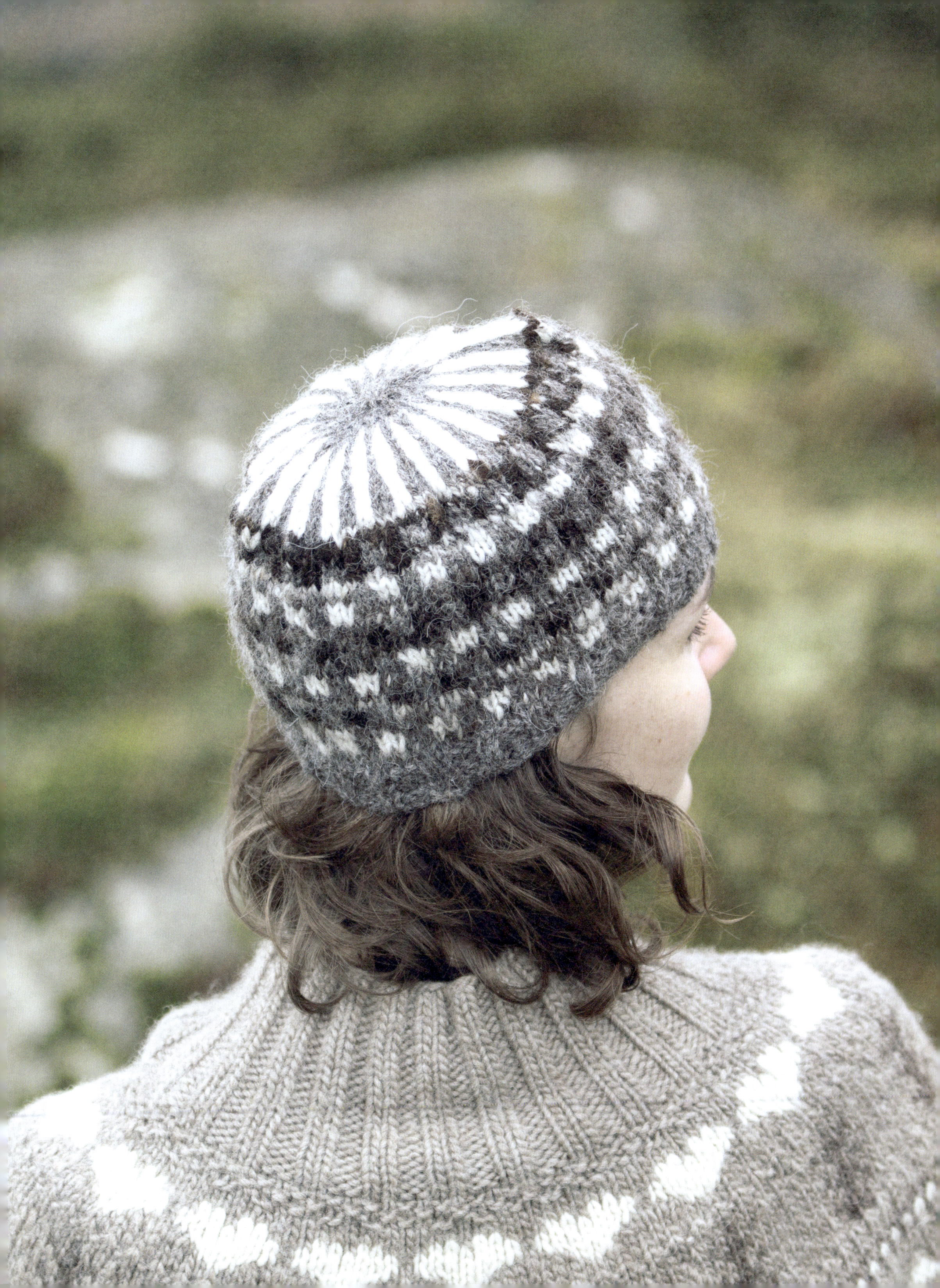

Instructions

Using 3.5mm (US 4) needles and MC, cast on 96 sts. Join ends to work in the round, making sure the work is not twisted. PM to denote EOR/BOR. At end of each rnd going forward, SM to ensure EOR/BOR position is not lost.

Rib

Work rib section following Chart A rows 1-8 or detailed instructions below:

Rib rnd 1 (RS): [K2, p2, LT, p2] to EOR.

Rep rnd 1 seven times more.

Body

Change to 4.5mm (US 7) needles and yarn CC3. Do not cut MC yarn. Carry unused yarn up as needed.

Working in stranded technique follow chart rows 9-34 using MC, CC1, CC2 and CC3 yarns as indicated

After rnd 34, cut both CC3 and CC2, leaving enough tail length to weave in ends.

Crown

Start shaping the crown following chart rows 35-48, or detailed instructions below:

Rnd 35 (RS): [With MC k2, with CC1 k2] to EOR.

Rnd 36-37: As Rnd 35.

Rnd 38: [With MC k2tog, with CC1 k2] to EOR. (72 sts)

Rnd 39-40: [With MC k1, with CC1 k2] to EOR.

Rnd 41: [With MC k1, with CC1 k2tog] to EOR. (48 sts)

Rnd 42-43: [With MC k1, with CC1 k1] to EOR.

Cut CC1, leaving enough tail length to weave in. Continue with MC only.

Rnd 44: K2tog to EOR. (24 sts)

Rnd 45: K to EOR.

Rnd 46: K2tog to EOR. (12 sts)

Cut MC leaving a tail of approximately 30cm (12in).

Finishing

Thread tapestry needle with the MC end and thread it through the rem 12 sts, removing them one by one from the knitting needle. Pull the end to tighten and close the hole at the top of the hat. Secure the end to ensure it can't loosen.

Weave in all ends.

Block for a professional finished look.

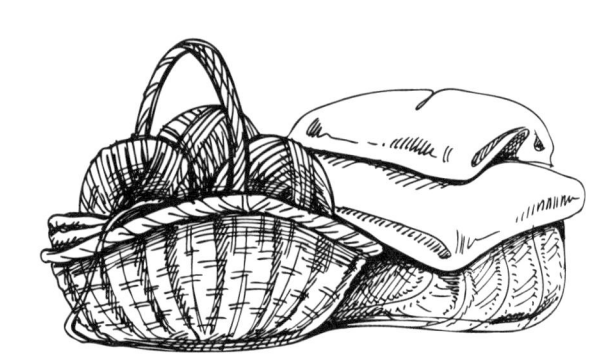

CHART A

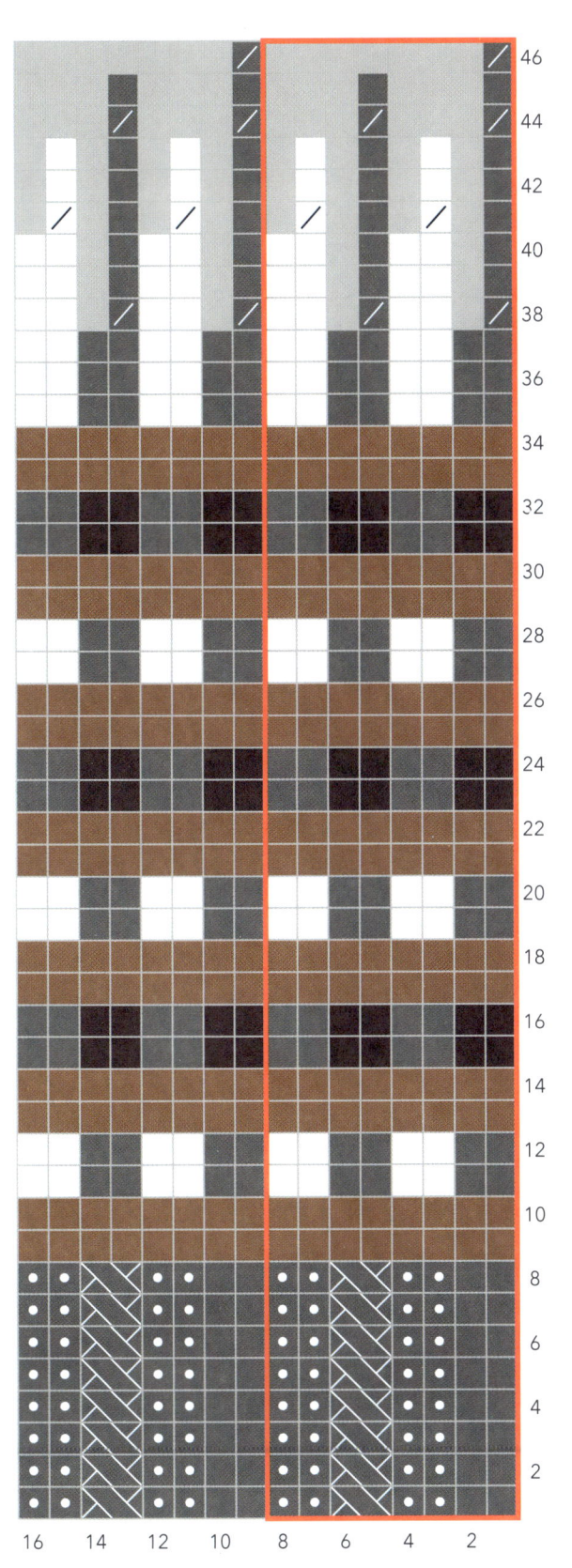

KEY

☐	Knit
•	Purl
⋈	LT
╱	K2tog
■ (dark grey)	MC: Medium Grey (006)
☐	CC1: Ecru (001)
■ (brown black)	CC2: Brown Black (007)
■ (brown)	CC3: Marl
▭ (orange outline)	Pattern repeat
■ (light grey)	Grey no stitch

Chart Note

Each square represents one stitch. The colour of the square denotes the shade of yarn to be used. A symbol inside the square indicates what action to work.

Atha Checkered Hat • 105

The Romney has Roman lineage, giving its fleece some natural lustre. This produces a soft, slightly shiny yarn that works well in plain knits. The Semo is a warm but light sweater, designed with plenty of ease, making it a comfortable wear that also looks expensive. The sheep that produced the yarn I've used were crossed with Shetlands, creating a premium-quality product.

Semo Sweater
in Romney

Pattern Notes

The Semo is an oversized high-neck style with an easy fit. The pattern is knitted bottom up, with the body and sleeves worked flat.

The main body and sleeves are knitted in stocking stitch with fashioning work at the front and back shoulders to create the raglan sleeves.

The sleeves have deep cuffs with an alternate rib and cable pattern. There's a simple 2x2 rib stitch around the hem.

The neck is knitted on circular needles after the body panels have been attached.

As this is an oversized style there are only two sizes: small/medium and large/X-large.

Skill level: for beginners to intermediate knitters

Materials

YARN
Romney X Shetland Shearling Wool (100% wool), 4-ply, 100g (250m/273yds). Supplied by Fernhill Fibre

Shade: Silver Mist; 650 (750)g; 7 (8) skeins with 2 strands held together throughout

NEEDLES
- 5mm (US 8) needles
- 4.5mm (US 7) 40cm (16in) circular needles or DPNs

OTHER
- Stitch holder

Tension (Gauge)

17 sts x 24 rows measures 10cm (4in) square over stocking stitch using 5mm (US 8) needles.

Sizes and Garment Measurements

(Measurements after blocking)

	SMALL/MEDIUM	LARGE/X-LARGE
To fit bust	81–97cm (32–38in)	102–117cm (40–46in)
Bust circumference	129cm (50¾in)	149cm (58¾in)
Length back hem to upper shoulder	61cm (24in)	63cm (24¾in)
Length from hem to underarm	35cm (13¾in)	36cm (14¼in)
Length from cuff to underarm	47cm (18½in)	49cm (19¼in)
Upper sleeve circumference	48cm (19in)	49cm (19¼in)

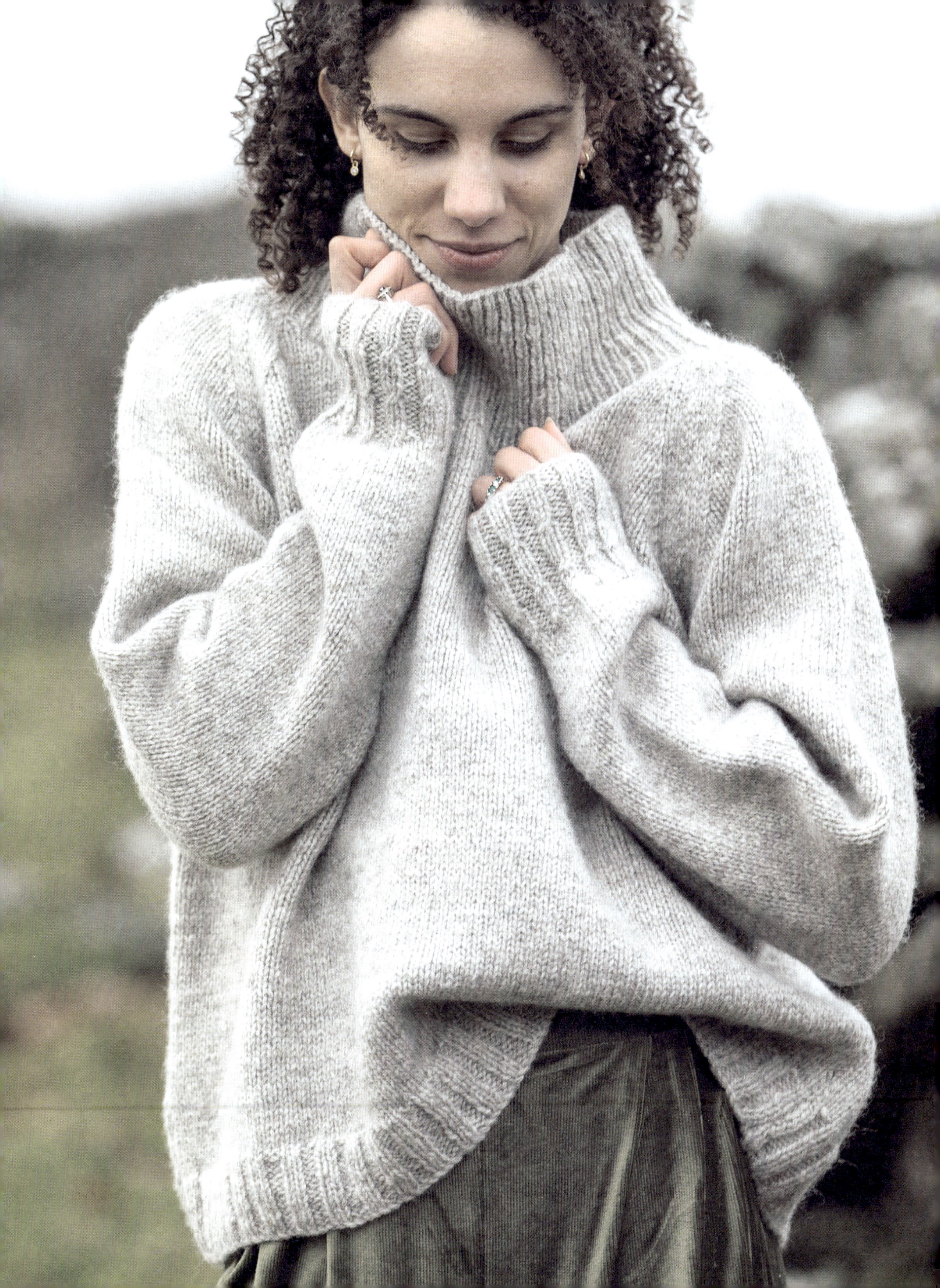

Instructions

Back

Using 5mm (US 8) needles and with 2 strands of yarn held together throughout, cast on 110 (126) sts.

Row 1 (WS): P2, [k2, p2] to end.

Row 2 (RS): K2, [p2, k2] to end.

Row 3 (WS): P2, [k2, p2] to end.

Rep last 2 rows four times more.

Next row (RS): K to end.

Next row (WS): P to end.

Above 2 rows define ss. Cont in ss until work measures 35 (36)cm (13¾ (14 ¼)in) from cast on edge, ending on WS row.

Back shaping of raglan and neckline

Cont in ss, AT THE SAME TIME, dec 1 st at each end of next 4 (16) rows, as follows:

RS Dec row (RS): K2, skpsso, k to last 4 sts, k2tog, k2.

WS Dec row (WS): P2, p2tog, p to last 4 sts, p2togtbl, p2. (102 (94) sts)

Next dec 1 st at each end of next row and following 28 (23) alt rows as RS dec row above.

(44 (46) sts)

Next row (WS): P to end.

Cast (bind) off.

Front

Using 5mm (US 8) needles work as given for back until Back Shape Raglan and Neckline.

Front shaping of raglan and neckline

Dec for raglan as in back until there are 68 (74) sts on needle at the end of a WS row.

To shape neckline and AT THE SAME TIME cont with the raglan shaping, work each side of neck separately starting with left side of neck then right side of neck.

Left side of neck

Next row (RS): K2, skpsso, k until there are 23 (24) sts on right needle, turn. Transfer rem 44 (49) sts onto a st holder. (23 (24) sts)

Dec 1 st at neck edge of next 5 rows, then on 2 alt rows, then on 3 fourth rows, at the same time shaping raglan, until there are 3 sts left on the needle. Detailed steps are as follows:

Shaping row 1 (WS): P2togtbl, p to end. (22 (23) sts)

Shaping row 2 (RS): K2, skpsso, k to last 2 sts, skpsso. (20 (21) sts)

Rep last 2 rows. (17 (18) sts)

Shaping row 5 (WS): P2togtbl, p to end. (16 (17) sts)

Shaping row 6 (RS): K2, skpsso, k to last 2 sts, skpsso. (14 (15) sts)

Shaping row 7 (WS): P to end.

Rep last 2 rows. (12 (13) sts)

Shaping row 10 (RS): K2, skpsso, k to last 2 sts, skpsso. (10 (11) sts)

Shaping row 11 (WS): P to end.

Shaping row 12 (RS): K2, skpsso, k to end. (9 (10) sts)

Shaping row 13 (WS): P to end.

Rep last 4 rows. (6 (7) sts)

Shaping row 18 (RS): K2, skpsso, k to last 2 sts, skpsso. (4 (5) sts)

Shaping row 19 (WS): P to end.

FOR SIZE S/M ONLY:

Shaping row 20 (RS): K2, skpsso. (3 (-) sts)

FOR SIZE L/XL ONLY:

Shaping row 20 (RS): K2, skpsso, k1. (- (4) sts)

Shaping row 21 (WS): P to end.

Shaping row 22 (RS): K2, skpsso. (- (3) sts)

BOTH SIZES:

Cast (bind) off.

Right side of neck

Transfer 44 (49) sts from st holder back onto working needle.

With RS facing, join yarn and cast (bind) off 20 (24) sts (representing front neckline centre st), k to last 4 sts, k2tog, k2. (23 (24) sts)

Dec 1 st on neck edge on the next 5 rows, then on 2 alt rows, then on 3 fourth rows, at the same time as shaping the raglan, until there are 3 sts left on the needle. Detailed steps are as follows:

Shaping row 1 (WS): P to last 2 sts, p2tog. (22 (23) sts)

Shaping row 2 (RS): K2tog, k to last 4 sts, k2tog, k2. (20 (21) sts)

Rep last 2 rows. (17 (18) sts)

Shaping row 5 (WS): P to last 2 sts, p2tog. (16 (17) sts)

Shaping row 6 (RS): K2tog, k to last 4 sts, k2tog, k2. (14 (15) sts)

Shaping row 7 (WS): P to end.

Rep last 2 rows. (12 (13) sts)

Shaping row 10 (RS): K2tog, k to last 4 sts, k2tog, k2. (10 (11) sts)

Shaping row 11 (WS): P to end.

Shaping row 12 (RS): K to last 4 sts, k2tog, k2. (9 (10) sts)

Shaping row 13 (WS): P to end.

Rep last 4 rows. (6 (7) sts)

Shaping row 18 (RS): K2tog, k to last 4 sts, k2tog, k2. (4 (5) sts)

Shaping row 19 (WS): P to end.

FOR SIZE S/M ONLY:

Shaping row 20 (RS): K2tog, k2. (3 (-) sts)

FOR SIZE L/XL ONLY:

Shaping row 20 (RS): K1, k2tog, k2. (- (4) sts)

Shaping row 21 (WS): P to end.

Shaping row 22 (RS): K2tog, k2. (- (3) sts)

BOTH SIZES:

Cast (bind) off.

Sleeves (make 2)

Using 5mm (US 8) needles and 2 strands of yarn held together throughout, cast on 44 sts.

Rib row 1 (RS): (K2, p2) to end.

Rib rows 2-8: As rib row 1.

Rib row 9: K2, p2, (RT, p2) to end.

Rib rows 10-16: As rib row 1.

Rib row 17: K2, p2, (RT, p2) to end.

Rib rows 18-24: As rib row 1.

Inc row (RS): K4, *RT, k2, M1R, (RT, k2) twice, rep from * to last 4 sts, M1R, RT, k2. (48 sts)

Next row (WS): P to end.

Work in ss throughout, AT THE SAME TIME, shape sleeve as follows:

Using the inc row instruction below, inc 1 st at each end of next row and 4 (5) following alt rows, then 12 following fourth rows until work measures 47 (49)cm (18½ (19¼)in) from cast on edge, ending on a WS row.

Inc row (RS): K1, M1L, k to last 2 sts, M1R, k1. (82 (84) sts)

Shape Raglan

Using the dec row instructions below, dec 1 st at each end of next 6 rows, then 28 (29) following alt rows as follows:

RS dec row (RS): K2, skpsso, k to last 4 sts, k2tog, k2. (2 sts dec)

WS dec row (WS): P2, p2tog, p to last 4 sts, p2togtbl, p2. (2 sts dec)

14 sts.

Cast (bind) off.

Assembly and finishing

For best results, use mattress st (see Special Techniques) for joining all seams.

Join sleeves to front piece along front raglan seams.

Join sleeves to back piece along back raglan seams.

Join back and front along side seam cont on to sleeve side seams.

Neckline trim

To work neckband, using 4.5mm (US 8) circular needles or DPNs pick up and knit 116 (120) sts along neckline as follows:

Starting from top of left back raglan seam pick up and knit:

10 sts along top of left sleeve from back left raglan seam to front left raglan seam.

60 (62) sts along front neckline from front left raglan seam to front right raglan seam.

10 sts along top of right sleeve from front right raglan seam to back right raglan seam.

36 (38) sts along back neckline from back right raglan seam to back left raglan seam.

Join in the round and work in k1, p1 rib for 29 rounds.

Cast (bind) off in rib pattern.

Weave in all ends.

Block for a professional finished look.

The regalness of the creamy-white Portland makes it the perfect sheep for creating a beautiful shawl. The dense fleece produces a yarn with a delicate and fluffy handle – although, as this is a primitive breed, it's still remarkably hard-wearing. This project combines traditional aran techniques with a modern paisley design. There's a hint of caramel in the sheep's coats that can also be seen in the finished shawl.

Malvina Shawl
in Portland

Pattern Notes

The luxurious Malvina shawl features paisley patterns made up of bobble stitches (see Special Techniques). It's worth practising this stitch before you start the project, to make sure you get the hang of increasing by knitting into the front and back of a stitch.

Around the hem, there's a pattern of rib, cables and garter stitches. All the detailed work is at the ends of the shawl, with plain stocking stitch in between.

The pattern is one size only.

Skill level: for intermediate to experienced knitters

Materials

YARN
Portland Wool (100% wool), 4-ply, 100g, (350m / 383 yds). Supplied by Armscote Manor

Shade: Natural white; 500g; 5 skeins

NEEDLES
- 3.75mm (US 5) needles

Tension (Gauge)

24 sts x 30 rows measures 10cm (4in) square over stocking stitch using 3.75mm (US 5) needles.

Garment Measurements

(Measurements after blocking)

Approximately 160 x 43cm (63 x 17in)

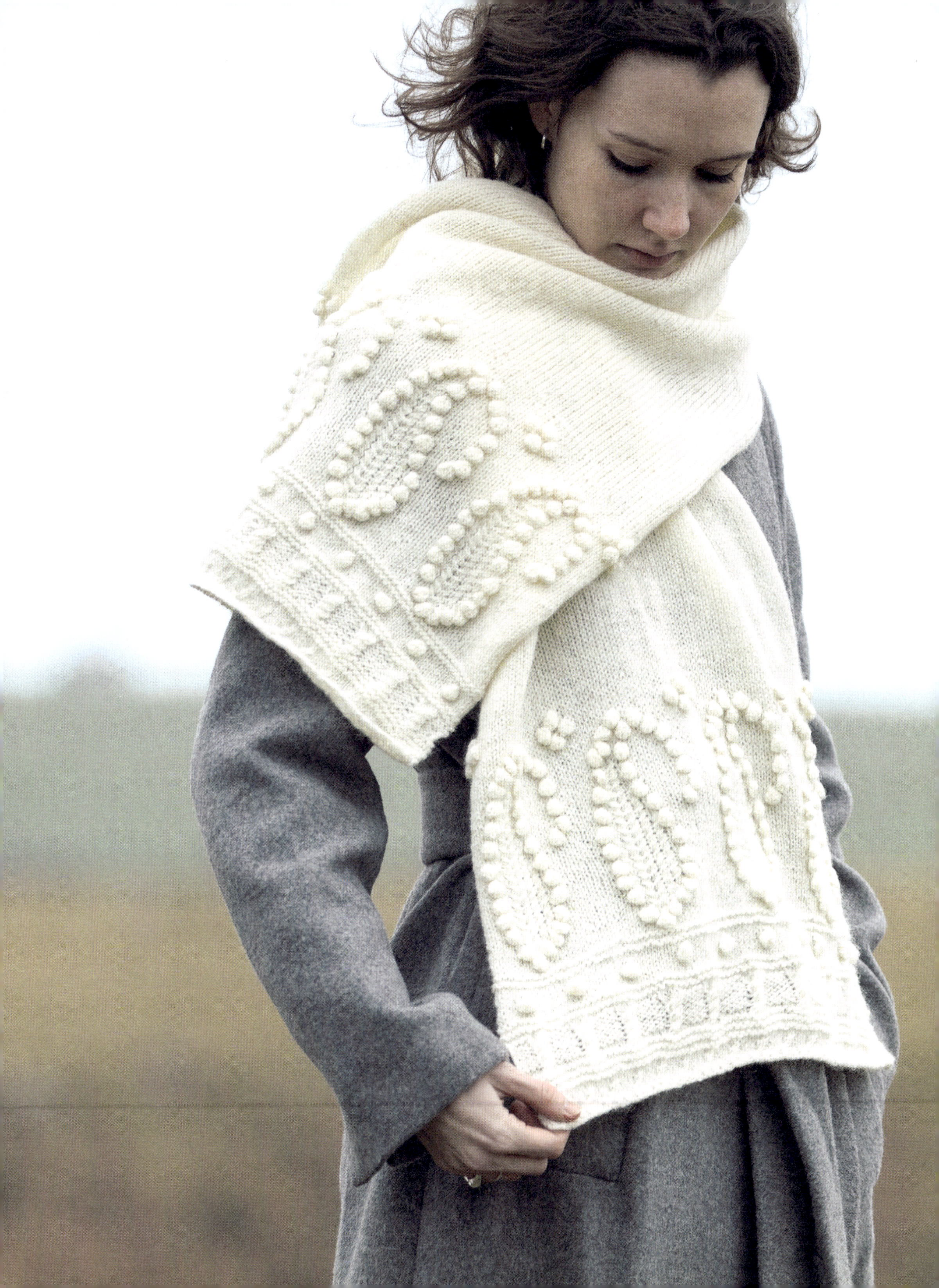

Instructions

Cast on 92 sts.

Rib section

Row 1 (RS): [K1, p1] to end.

Rep row 1.

Right twist section

Row 1 (RS): [K3, RT] to last 2 st, k2.

Row 2 (WS): P to end.

Row 3: K2, RT, [k3, RT] to last 3 sts, k3.

Row 4: P to end.

Row 5: K1, RT, [k3, RT] to last 4 sts, k4.

Row 6: P to end.

Garter divider 1

Work 4 rows of p.

Cable section

Row 1 (RS): P4, [k4, p4] to end.

Rows 2, 4, 6 (WS): K4, [p4, k4] to end.

Row 3: P4, [C4B, p4] to end.

Row 5: P4, [k4, p4] to end.

Row 7: P4, [C4B, p4] to end.

Rows 8: K4, [p4, k4] to end.

Garter divider 2

Work 4 rows of k.

Bobble border section

Row 1 (RS): K to end.

Row 2 (WS): P to end.

Above 2 rows define ss pattern.

Work 2 rows more of ss.

Row 5: K5, [Bb, K8] 9 times, Bb, k5.

Row 6: P to end.

Work 2 rows of ss.

Garter divider 3

Work 4 rows of k.

Paisley design border section

Work 2 rows of ss.

Follow Chart A to work the paisley design or follow detailed instructions below:

Row 1 (RS): K7, [k11, Bb, K9] 4 times, k1.

Row 2 and all WS rows to row 48 (WS): P to end.

Row 3: K7, [k9, Bb, RT, k1, Bb, k7] 4 times, k1.

Row 5: K7, [k7, Bb, RT twice, LT, k7] 4 times, k1.

Row 7: K7, [k6, Bb, k1, RT twice, LT, k1, Bb, k5] 4 times, k1.

Row 9: K7, [k5, Bb, RT 3 times, LT twice, k5] 4 times, k1.

Row 11: K7, [k6, RT 3 times, LT twice, Bb, k4] 4 times, k1.

Row 13: K7, [k4, Bb, k1, RT 3 times, LT twice, Bb, k4] 4 times, k1.

Row 15: K7, [k6, RT 3 times, LT twice, k5] 4 times, k1.

Row 17: As row 13.

Row 19: As row 15.

Row 21: K7, [k5, Bb, RT 3 times, LT twice, Bb, k4] 4 times, k1.

Row 23: K7, [k8, RT twice, LT, k7] 4 times, k1.

Row 25: K7, [k1, Bb, k4, Bb, k1, RT twice, LT, k1, Bb, k5] 4 times, k1.

Row 27: K7, [Bb, k7, RT twice, LT, k7] 4 times, k1.

Row 29: K7, [k7, Bb, RT twice, LT, Bb, k6] 4 times, k1.

Row 31: K7, [Bb, k9, RT, LT, k7] 4 times, k1.

Row 33: K7, [k8, Bb, k1, RT, k1, Bb, k7] 4 times, k1.

Row 35: K7, [Bb, k9, RT, k9] 4 times, k1.

Row 37: K7, [k8, Bb, k3, Bb, k8] 4 times, k1.

Row 39: K7, [k1, Bb, k9, Bb, k9] 4 times, k1.

Row 41: K7, [k3, Bb, k3, Bb, k2, Bb, k10] 4 times, k1.

Row 43: K4, Bb, k2, [k5, Bb, k2, Bb, k8, Bb, k3] 4 times, k1.

Row 45: K2, Bb, k3, Bb, [k15, Bb, k3, Bb, k1] 4 times, k1.

Row 47: K4, Bb, k2, [k17, Bb, k3] 4 times, k1.

Body

Cont in ss until work measures 130cm (51in) from cast on edge, ending on a WS row.

Reverse paisley design border section

Follow Chart B to work the paisley design or follow the detailed instructions below:

Row 1 (RS): K4, Bb, k2, [k17, Bb, k3] 4 times, k1.

Row 2 and all WS rows to row 48 (WS): P to end.

Row 3: K2, Bb, k3, Bb, [k15, Bb, k3, Bb, k1] 4 times, k1.

Row 5: K4, Bb, k2, [k5, Bb, k2, Bb, k8, Bb, k3] 4 times, k1.

Row 7: K7, [k3, Bb, k3, Bb, k2, Bb, k10] 4 times, k1.

Row 9: K7, [k1, Bb, k9, Bb, k9] 4 times, k1.

Row 11: K7, [k8, Bb, k3, Bb, k8] 4 times, k1.

Row 13: K7, [Bb, k9, RT, k9] 4 times, k1.

Row 15: K7, [k8, Bb, k1, RT, k1, Bb, k7] 4 times, k1.

Row 17: K7, [Bb, k9, RT, LT, k7] 4 times, k1.

Row 19: K7, [k7, Bb, RT twice, LT, Bb, k6] 4 times, k1.

Row 21: K7, [Bb, k7, RT twice, LT, k7] 4 times, k1.

Row 23: K7, [k1, Bb, k4, Bb, k1, RT twice, LT, k1, Bb, k5] 4 times, k1.

Row 25: K7, [k8, RT twice, LT, k7] 4 times, k1.

Row 27: K7, [k5, Bb, RT 3 times, LT twice, Bb, k4] 4 times, k1.

Row 29: K7, [k6, RT 3 times, LT twice, k5] 4 times, k1.

Row 31: K7, [k4, Bb, k1, RT 3 times, LT twice, Bb, k4] 4 times, k1.

Row 33: As row 29.

Row 35: As row 31.

Row 37: K7, [k6, RT 3 times, LT twice, Bb, k4] 4 times, k1.

Row 39: K7, [k5, Bb, RT 3 times, LT twice, k5] 4 times, k1.

Row 41: K7, [k6, Bb, k1, RT twice, LT, k1, Bb, k5] 4 times, k1.

Row 43: K7, [k7, Bb, RT twice, LT, k7] 4 times, k1.

Row 45: K7, [k9, Bb, RT, k1, Bb, k7] 4 times, k1.

Row 47: K7, [k11, Bb, K9] 4 times, k1.

Work 2 rows of ss.

Work Garter Divider 3 section.

Work Bobble Border section.

Work Garter Divider 2 section.

Work Cable section.

Work Garter Divider 1 section.

Work Right Twist section.

Work Rib section.

Cast (bind) off in rib pattern.

Weave in all ends.

Block for a professional finished look.

CHART A: PAISLEY DESIGN BORDER SECTION

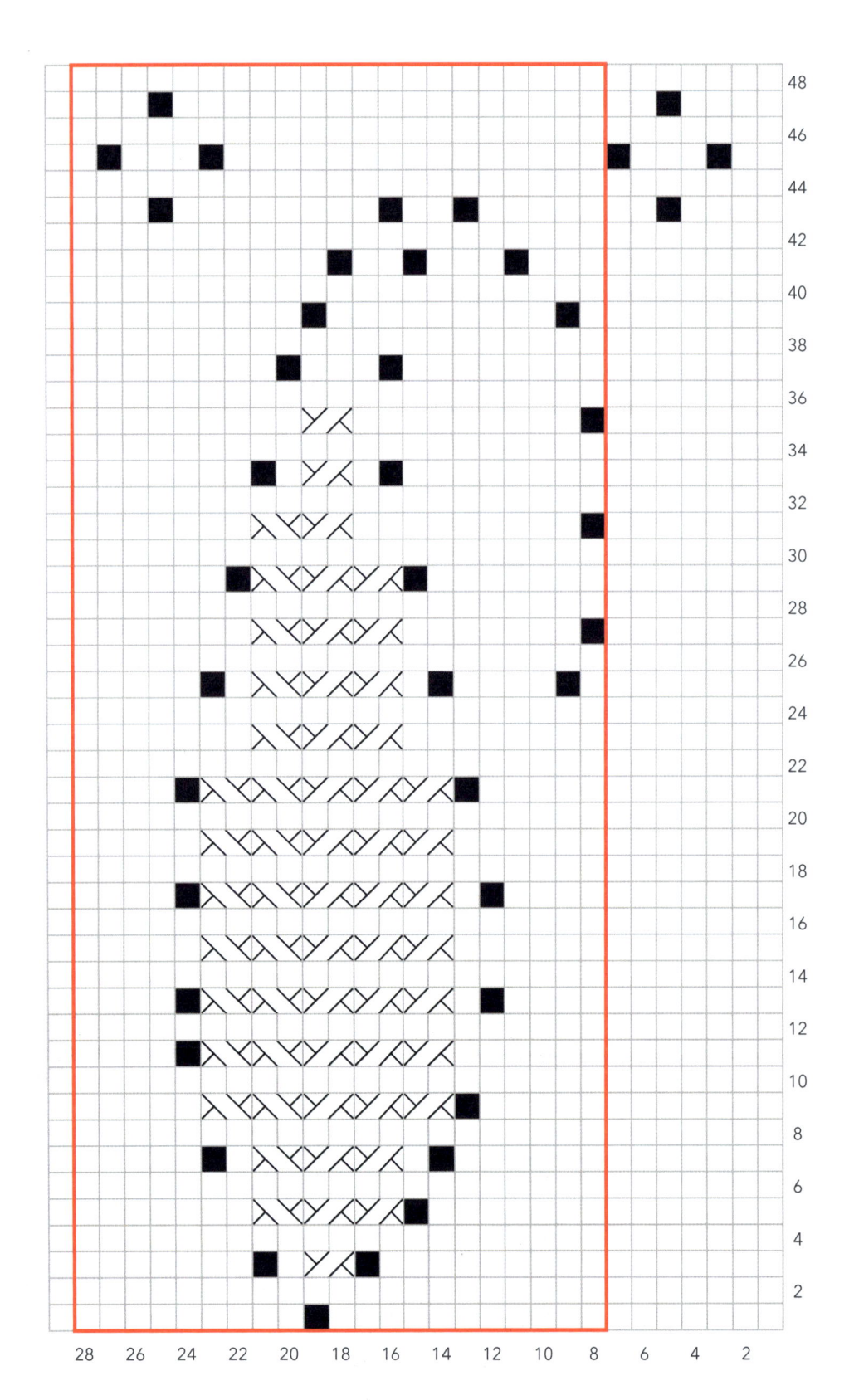

KEY

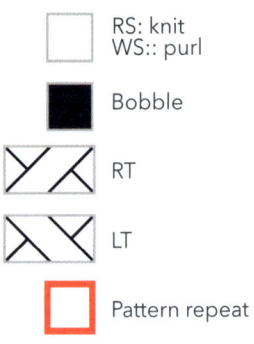

- ☐ RS: knit / WS: purl
- ■ Bobble
- ⧖ RT
- ⧗ LT
- ▢ Pattern repeat

Chart Note

Each square represents one stitch. A symbol inside the square indicates what action to work.

118 · Malvina Shawl

CHART B: REVERSE PAISLEY DESIGN BORDER SECTION

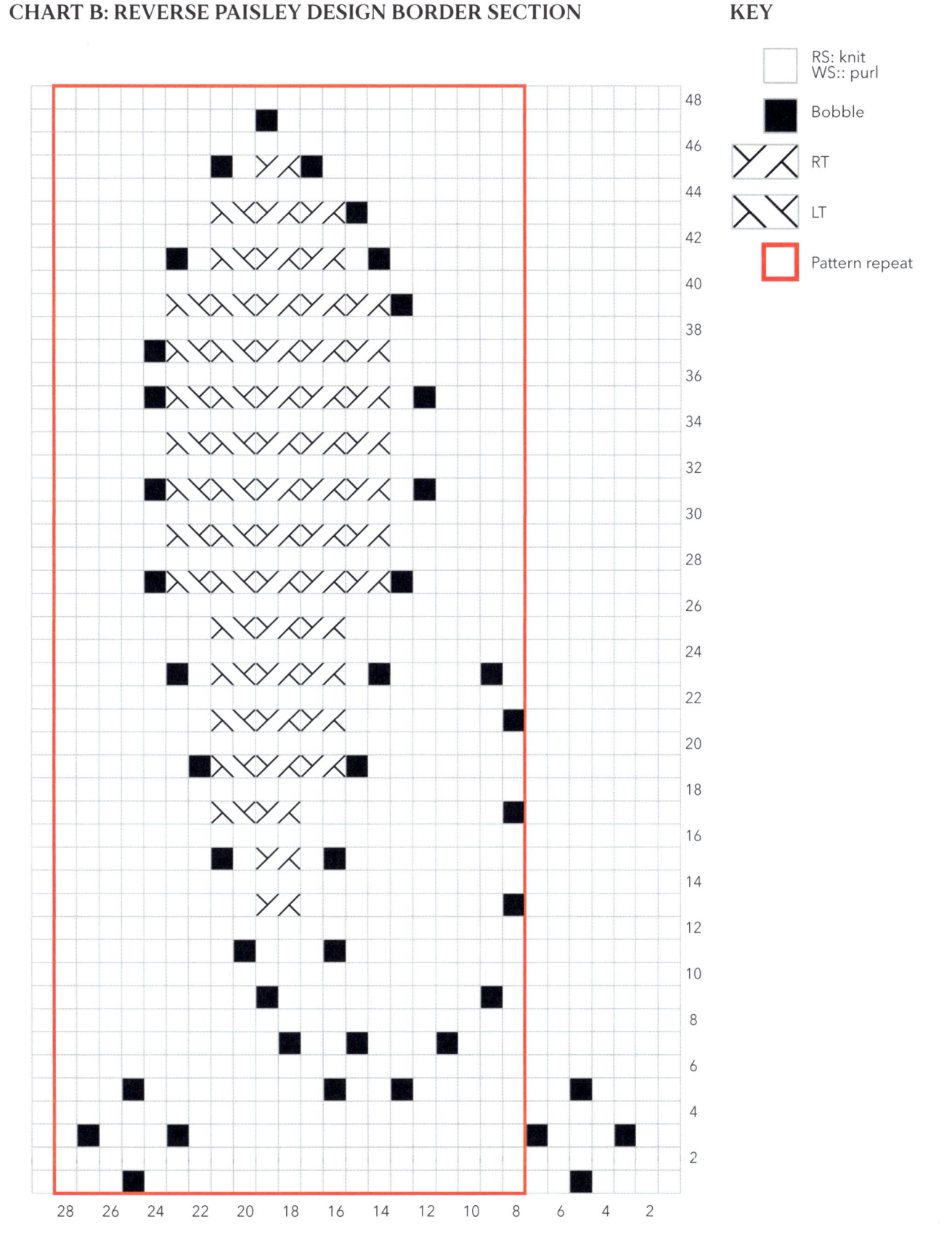

KEY

- ☐ RS: knit / WS: purl
- ■ Bobble
- RT
- LT
- ☐ Pattern repeat

Malvina Shawl • 119

The Cheviot has been bred to withstand the harsh winters of Scotland, so produces a fine, soft wool that's an excellent insulator. The Fair Isle design of this sweater uses many of the North Country Cheviot's natural colours – which range from white, soft and mid-grey, through to black and marl (which combines black and white). As the yarn is woollen spun, it creates a jumper that's both light to wear and extremely warm.

Orla Paisley Intarsia Sweater in Cheviot

Pattern Notes

This stylish sweater has raglan sleeves and a slash neck. Fair Isle colourwork on the hem and cuffs is achieved using the stranded knitting technique, where unused strands of yarn are carried across the wrong side of the work. The front central patterning is intarsia, so the yarn is only carried across the patterned section.

The construction of this garment is bottom up, with the front and back worked flat and separately, up to the underarms. The sleeves are worked in the round up to the underarms. Then all pieces (back, front and sleeves) are worked in the round to the neck on circular or double-pointed needles.

The pattern is for five sizes: small, medium, large, X-large, and XX-large.

Skill level: for experienced knitters

Materials

YARN

Machine Spun 4-ply (100% wool), 4-ply, 100g (350m/383yds). Supplied by Heatherlea Black Cheviot

Main colour: Grey Mouse Undyed; 350 (350) (400) (400) (450)g; 4 (4) (4) (4) (5) balls

Contrast colour 1: Shadow Undyed; 50g; 1 ball

Contrast colour 2: Marl Light Undyed; 50g; 1 ball

Contrast colour 3: Seal Grey Undyed; 50g; 1 ball

Contrast colour 4: White Undyed; 50g; 1 ball

NEEDLES

- 3.25 mm (US 3) circular needles
- 2.75 mm (US 2) circular needles or DPNs for neckline
- Cable needle

OTHER

- Stitch markers
- 3 stitch holders or stitch wires to hold front body, back body, and sleeve sts

Tension (Gauge)

24 sts x 35 rows measures 10cm 4in square over stocking stitch and stranded colourwork using 3.25mm (US 3) needles. Your tension when working stranded colourwork can be tighter than when working stocking stitch. Make sure to swatch for both stitch patterns. If there is a difference in tension, adjust needle sizes accordingly.

Sizes and Garment Measurements

(Measurements after blocking)

	SMALL	MEDIUM	LARGE	X-LARGE	XX-LARGE
To fit bust	81–86cm (32–34in)	92–97cm (36–38in)	102–107cm (40–42in)	112–117cm (44–46in)	122–127cm (48–50in)
Bust circumference	93cm (36½in)	103cm (40½in)	113cm (44½in)	123cm (48½in)	133cm (52½in)
Length from hem to underarm	34cm (13¼in)	35cm (13¾in)	36cm (14in)	37cm (14½in)	37cm (14½in)
Length from hem to upper shoulder	57cm (22½in)	60cm (23½in)	63cm (23¾in)	66cm (26in)	68cm (27in)
Sleeve length from cuff to underarm	45cm (17¾in)	46cm (18in)	47cm (18½in)	48cm (19in)	48cm (19in)
Upper sleeve circumference	38cm (15in)	40cm (15¾in)	42cm (16½in)	44cm (17½in)	46cm (18in)

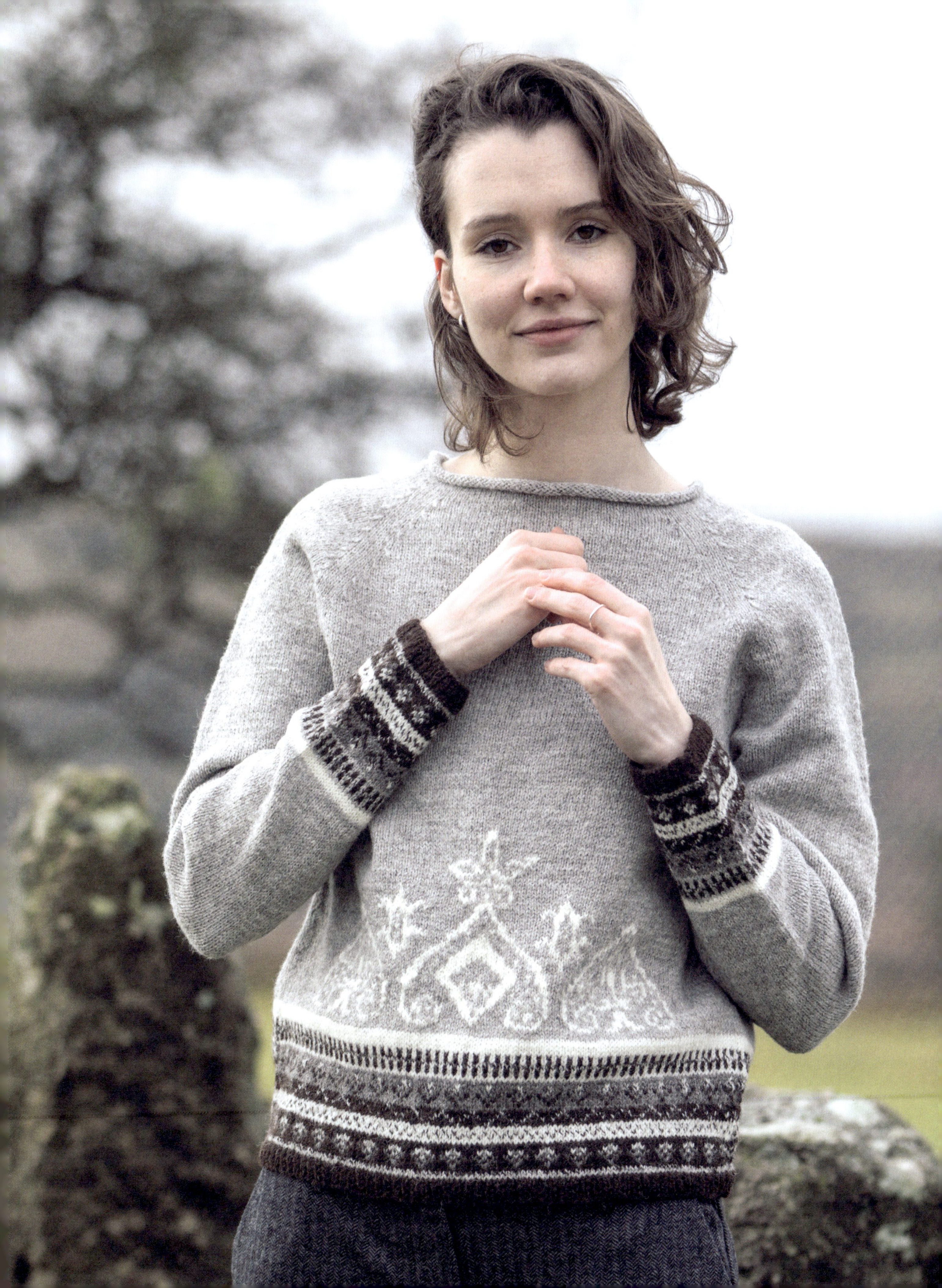

Instructions

Back

Using 3.5mm (US 3) needles and CC1, cast on 114 (126) (138) (150) (162) sts.

Rib row 1 (RS): [K1, p1] to end.

Rib row 2 (WS): [K1, p1] to end.

Rep above 2 rib rows twice more for a total of 6 rib rows.

Change to MC.

Work in ss following Chart A until all rows are worked, changing yarn where indicated in chart.

Cut all but MC yarn, leaving long enough tails to weave in ends.

Cont with MC in ss until work measures 34 (35) (36) (37) (37)cm (13¼ (13¾) (14) (14½) (14½)in) from cast on edge, ending on a WS row.

Cast (bind) off 6 (7) (8) (9) (11) sts for armhole, k to last 6 (7) (8) (9) (11) sts, cast (bind) off last 6 (7) (8) (9) (11) sts for other armhole. Cut yarn, leaving long enough tail to weave in. (102 (112) (122) (132) (140) sts)

Transfer all live sts to a st holder, st wire or equivalent.

Front

Work as Back until end of Chart A.

With MC yarn, work 2 rows of ss.

Cont in ss, AT THE SAME TIME incorporate Chart B as follows:

Row 39 (RS): K10 (16) (22) (28) (34), PM, work row 1 Chart B, PM, k to end.

Row 40 (WS): P to marker, SM, work row 2 Chart B, SM, p to end.

Row 41: K to marker, SM, work row 3 Chart B, SM, k to end.

Row 42: P to marker, SM, work row 4 Chart B, SM, p to end.

Cont as above until all rows in Chart B are worked.

Cut CC4, leaving a long enough tail to weave in end. Remove markers.

Cont with MC in ss until work measures 34 (35) (36) (37) (37)cm (13¼ (13¾) (14) (14½) (14½)in) from cast on edge, ending on a WS row.

Cast (bind) off 6 (7) (8) (9) (11) sts for armhole, k to last 6 (7) (8) (9) (11) sts, cast (bind) off last 6 (7) (8) (9) (11) sts for other armhole. Cut yarn, leaving a long enough tail to weave in end. (102 (112) (122) (132) (140) sts)

Transfer all live sts to a st holder, st wire or equivalent.

Sleeves (make 2)

Using 3.5mm (US 3) needles and CC1, cast on 56 (58) (58) (60) (60) sts.

Join both ends to work in the rnd, making sure the work is not twisted. PM to denote BOR/EOR.

Rib rnd 1 (RS): [K1, p1] to EOR.

Rep rib rnd 1 four times more.

FOR SIZE S ONLY:

Rib rnd 6: K1, pfb, [k1, p1] 6 times, k1, pfb, [k1, p1] 6 times, k1, pfb, [k1,p1] 6 times, k1, pfb, [k1, p1] to EOR. (4 sts inc)

FOR SIZES M, L ONLY:

Rib rnd 6: K1, pfb, [k1, p1] 13 times, k1, pfb, [k1, p1] to EOR. (2 sts inc)

FOR SIZES XL, XXL ONLY:

Rib rnd 6: *K1, pfb, [k1, p1] 4 times**, rep from * to ** 5 times. (6 sts inc)

There should be 60 (60) (60) (66) (66) sts on needle.

Using MC work in ss following Chart C for colourwork until all Chart C rows are worked, changing yarn as specified. AT THE SAME TIME, inc 1 st at each end of a rnd every 7 rnds as shown in Chart C. Inc rnds are worked as follows: K1, M1L, work per corresponding chart row until last 2 sts, M1R, k1.

At end of Chart C, there should be 68 (68) (68) (74) (74) sts on the needle.

Change to MC.

Work the rest of the sleeves in MC only. AT THE SAME TIME, inc in the same way as before on next and every following 9th (8th) (7th) (7th) (6th) rnd until there are 92 (96) (100) (106) (112) sts on the needle.

Cont in ss until work measures 45 (46) (47) (48) (48)cm (17¾ (18) (18½) (19) (19)in) from cuff cast on edge.

On the last rnd, k to last 5 (6) (7) (8) (10) sts, cast (bind) off 10 (12) (14) (16) (20) sts for armhole removing st marker, k to end. (82 (84) (86) (90) (92) sts)

For 1st sleeve, transfer sts to a st holder, st wire or equivalent. Cut yarn, leaving a long enough tail to weave in.

For 2nd sleeve, leave sts on working needle, do not cut yarn.

Yoke

Yoke is worked in the rnd with back centre being start/end of rnd.

SET UP:

Transfer Back sts onto the other needle so they are ready to be worked on with RS facing.

Hold needle carrying 2nd sleeve sts as working needle, k51 (56) (61) (66) (70) sts of back, PM to mark BOR/EOR at centre of back, k rem 51 (56) (61) (66) (70) sts, PM to mark back left raglan position.

Transfer first sleeve sts onto the other needle so they are ready to be worked on with RS facing.

K82 (84) (86) (90) (92) sts (all first sleeve sts), PM to mark front left raglan position.

Next, transfer Front sts onto the other needle so they are ready to be worked on with RS facing.

K102 (112) (122) (132) (140) sts (all front sts), PM to mark front right raglan position.

Join to second sleeve sts to complete round, k82 (84) (86) (90) (92) sts (all second sleeve sts), PM to mark back right raglan position, k to EOR.

368 (392) (416) (444) (464) sts.

Work 14 (12) (10) (5) (1) rnds of ss, always slipping st markers to retain markers' positions.

Next, start shaping raglan.

FOR SIZES M, XL AND XXL ONLY:

Shape by dec body side but not sleeve side of raglan as follows:

Rnd 1: *K to 5 sts before next marker, ssk, k3, SM, k to next marker, SM, k3, k2tog, rep from *, k to EOR. (-- (388) (--) (440) (460) sts)

Rnd 2: *K to 4 sts before next marker, ssk, k2, SM, k to next marker, SM k2, k2tog, rep from *, k to EOR. (-- (384) (--) (436) (456) sts)

Rnd 3: K to EOR.

Rnd 4: K to EOR.

FOR ALL SIZES:

Cont with raglan shaping by decreasing body and sleeve sides of raglan as follows:

Rnd 1: *K to 5 sts before next marker, ssk, k3, SM, k3, k2tog**, rep from * to ** 3 times more, k to EOR. (8 sts dec)

Rnd 2: *K to 4 sts before next marker, ssk, k2, SM, k2, k2tog**, rep from * to ** 3 times more, k to EOR. (8 sts dec)

Rnd 3: K to EOR.

Rnd 4: K to EOR.

Rep the above 4 rnds for all sizes until 128 (128) (128) (132) (136) sts left on needles at end of Rnd 4. That is working the above four rnds 15 (16) (18) (19) (20) times in total.

Work German short rows (see Special techniques) for a raised back neck as follows:

Next row (RS): K38 (38) (38) (41) (44), turn.

Next row (WS): Wyif sl1p and make DS, p to EOR, SM, p38 (38) (38) (41) (44), turn.

Next row (RS): Wyif sl1p and make DS, k to EOR, SM, k to 5 sts before DS created in previous RS row, turn.

Next row (WS): Wyif sl1p and make DS, p to EOR, SM, k to 5 sts before DS created in previous WS row, turn.

Rep last 2 rows 1 (1) (2) (2) (2) times more.

Next, wyif sl1p and make DS, k to EOR.

Resume working in the rnd. K one rnd making sure each DS is worked as 1 st.

Neck

Change to 2.75mm (US 2) needles.

Work 8 rnds of ss. Cast (bind) off.

Assembly and finishing

Join front and back sides by sewing using mattress stitch in the ditch between the edge sts and the next sts of each piece. The ditch is the area between 2 adjacent stitches.

Sew underarm of each sleeve hole using mattress stitch.

Weave in all ends.

Block for a professional finished look.

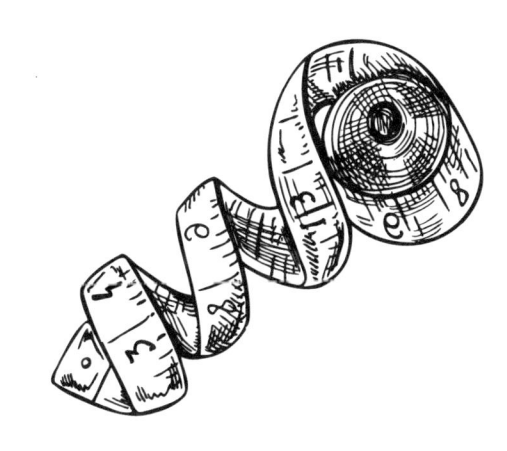

CHART A: BACK AND FRONT

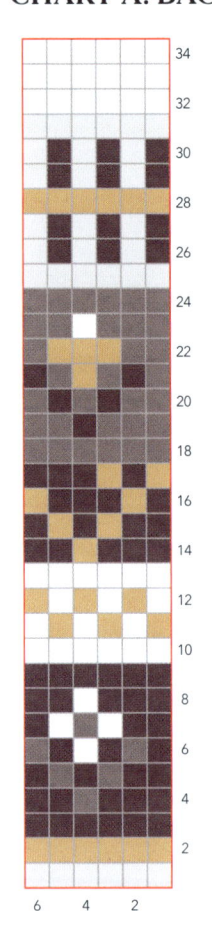

Chart Note

Each square represents one stitch. The colour of the square denotes what yarn shade to use. A symbol inside the square indicates what action to work.

CHART B: CONE MOTIF

CHART A KEY

- MC: Grey mouse undyed
- CC1: Shadow undyed
- CC2: Marl light undyed
- CC3: Seal grey undyed
- CC4: White undyed
- Pattern repeat

CHART B KEY

- MC – Grey mouse undyed
- CC4 – White undyed

126 · Orla Paisley Intarsia Sweater

CHART C: CUFF

CHART C KEY

- ☐ MC: Grey mouse undyed
- ■ CC1: Shadow undyed
- ■ CC2: Marl light undyed
- ■ CC3: Seal grey undyed
- ☐ CC4: White undyed
- ʎ M1L – left-leaning increase
- ʏ M1R – right-leaning increase
- ▭ Pattern repeat
- ■ No stitch

Orla Paisley Intarsia Sweater • 127

While visiting the Wool Board's depot in Bradford, I came across a big pile of jet-black fleece. It was so soft, I asked which breed it was, and was told it was Black Welsh Mountain lambswool. This prompted a year-long search for this uniquely coloured yarn. Although now available, it's very rare – but worth searching out. With a shirt worn underneath, the sweater can easily be dressed up with statement jewellery. The kimono style, with its wider sleeves, brings a modern twist.

Ullin Sweater
in Black Welsh Mountain

Pattern Notes

The Ullin is a boxy-shaped, slash-neck sweater with dropped shoulders and wide sleeves.

This is a simple pattern with only two stitches – knit and purl – so it's a good option for beginners or anyone looking for a relaxing project.

The construction is flat, bottom up and the trims, hem, and cuffs are knitted in an extra-wide rib pattern. The textured front, back and sleeves are all knitted using purl stitch to define the horizontal and vertical stripes. These can be used to count rows to the armholes and shoulder points. The rolled neckline is worked in the round.

The pattern is for three sizes: small, medium, and large.

Skill level: for beginners through to experienced knitters

Materials

YARN
Black Welsh Mountain DK Yarn (100% wool), DK, 100g (265m/290yds). Supplied by SortTraeStudio

Shade: Natural black; 450 (500) (550)g; 5 (5) (6) skeins

NEEDLES
- 4mm (US 6) needles
- 3.25mm (US 3) circular needles or DPNs
- Tapestry needle

OTHER
- 1 stitch marker
- 2 stitch holders

Tension (Gauge)

19.5 sts x 30 rows measures 10cm (4in) square over stocking stitch using 4mm (US 6) needles.

Sizes and Garment Measurements

(Measurements after blocking)

	SMALL	MEDIUM	LARGE
To fit bust	88-91cm (34½-36in)	92-98cm (36-38½in)	104-109cm (41-43in)
Bust circumference	100cm (39¼in)	110cm (43¼in)	120cm (47¼in)
Length from hem to underarm	36cm (14in)	36cm (14in)	36cm (14in)
Length from hem to upper shoulder	56cm (22in)	57cm (22½in)	58cm (23in)
Length from hem to lower shoulder	53cm (21in)	54cm 21¼in)	55cm 21½in)
Sleeve underarm length	39cm (15¼in)	40cm (15¾in)	41cm (16in)
Sleeve length from cuff to lower shoulder	41cm (16in)	42cm (16½in)	43cm (17in)
Upper sleeve circumference	39cm (15¼in)	41cm (16in)	43cm (17in)

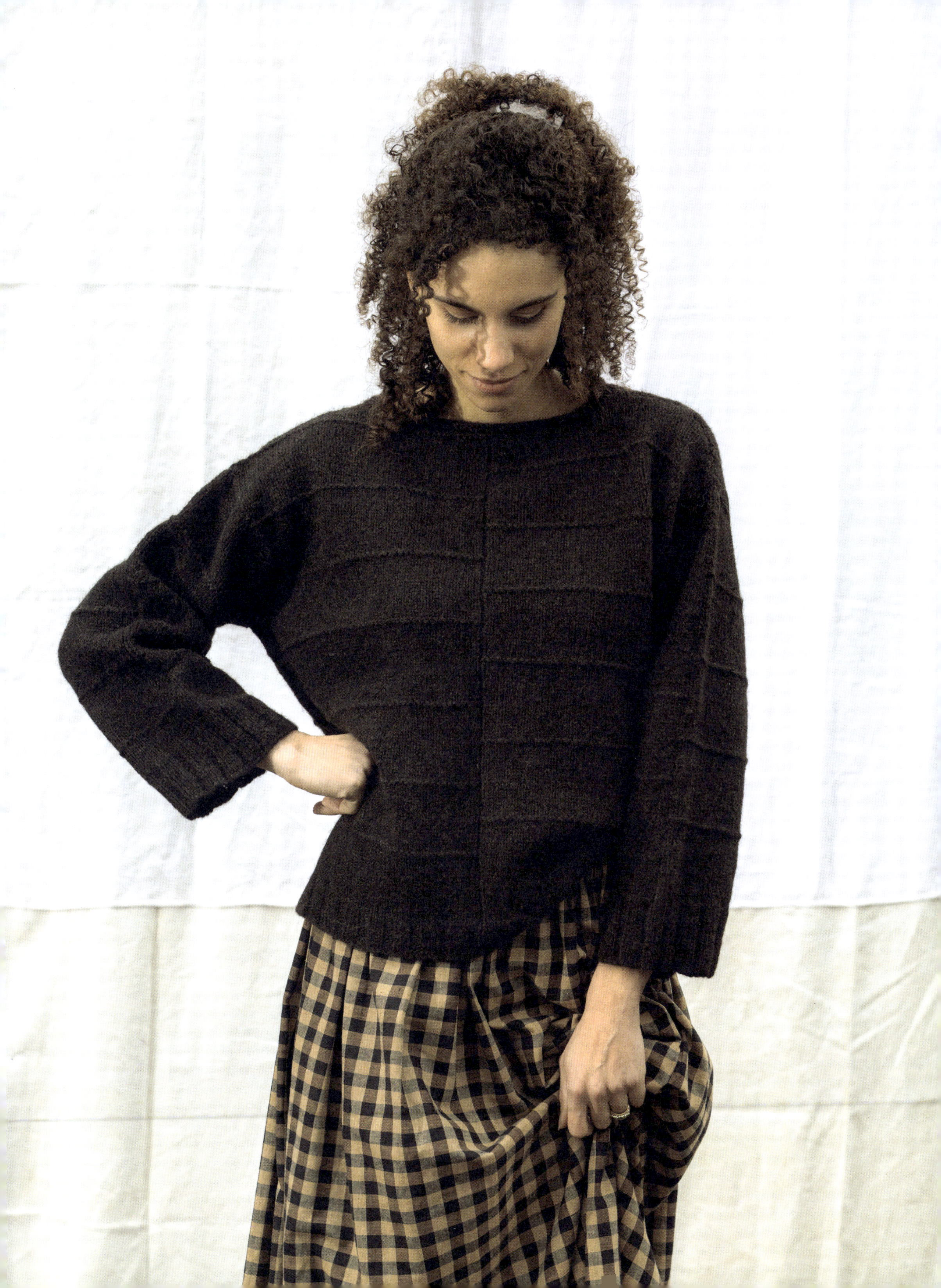

Instructions

Back

Using 6mm (US 6) needles, cast on 100 (105) (110) sts.

Rib row 1 (RS): [K3, p2] to end.

Rib row 2 (WS): [K2, p3] to end.

Rep Rib rows 1 and 2 eight times more.

Setup row 1 (RS): K49 (52) (54), PM, p1, k to end.

Setup row 2 (WS): P to 1 st before marker, k1, SM, p to end.

Row 1 (RS): K to marker, SM, p1, k to end.

Row 2 and all WS rows to row 22 (WS): P to one st before marker, k1, SM, p to end.

Rows 3, 5, 7, 9: As row 1.

Row 11: K to marker, SM, p to end.

Rows 13, 15, 17, 19: As row 1.

Row 21: P to marker, SM, p1, k to end.

Row 22: As row 2.

Rows 1-22 define the repeat st pattern for the back.

Cont working in this st pattern throughout until work measures 36cm (14in) from cast on edge, ending on a WS row.

Armhole shaping

Note: Whenever the pattern refers to right or left shoulder it is from perspective of the person wearing the piece not from the knitter's perspective facing the piece.

Using dec instruction below, dec 1 st at beg and end of the next and following 3 alt rows while maintaining st pattern:

Dec row: K1, ssk, work as per st pattern to last 3 sts, k2tog, k1. (92 (97) (102) sts)

Following st pattern cont straight until work measures 53 (54) (55)cm (21 (21¼) (21½)in) from cast on edge, ending on a WS row.

SHAPE SHOULDERS AND BACK NECKLINE:

Cast (bind) off 4 (5) (6) sts at the start of next 2 rows working rest of row as per pattern. (84 (87) (90) sts)

Cast (bind) off 5 sts at the start of next 2 rows working rest of row as per pattern. (74 (77) (80) sts)

Cast (bind) off 5 sts at the start of next 2 rows working rest of row as per pattern. (64 (67) (70) sts)

Work each side of back neck separately starting with right shoulder (see Note) as follows:

Next row (RS): Cast (bind) off 5 sts, work as per pattern until there are 7 (8) (8) sts on the right needle, turn, leaving rem 52 (54) (57) sts on a st holder.

Next row (WS): P2togtbl, work as per pattern to end. (6 (7) (7) sts)

Next row (RS): Work as per pattern to last 2 sts, ssk. (5 (6) (6) sts)

Cast (bind) off all 5 (6) (6) sts.

Return to the sts on st holder, leave the centre 40 (41) (44) sts on st holder and transfer last 12 (13) (13) sts onto the needle.

With RS facing, rejoin yarn and work on the left shoulder sts as follows:

Next row (RS): Work as per pattern to end. (12 (13) (13) sts)

Next row (WS): Cast (bind) off 5 sts, work to last 2 sts from end, p2tog. (6 (7) (7) sts)

Next row (RS): K2tog, k to end. (5 (6) (6) sts)

Cast (bind) off all 5 (6) (6) sts.

Front

Cast on and work as given for back up to and including Setup row 2.

Row 1 (RS): K to marker, SM, p1, k to end.

Row 2 and all WS rows to row 22 (WS): P to one st before marker, k1, SM, p to end.

Rows 3, 5, 7, 9: As row 1.

Row 11: P to marker, SM, p1, k to end.

Rows 13, 15, 17, 19: As row 1.

Row 21: K to marker, SM, p to end.

Rows 1-22 define the repeat st pattern for the front.

Cont working in this st pattern throughout front until work measures 36cm (14in) from cast on edge, ending on a WS row.

132 • Ullin Sweater

Armhole shaping

Using dec instruction below, dec 1 st at beg and end of the next and following 3 alt rows while maintaining st pattern:

Dec row: K1, ssk, work as per st pattern to last 3 sts, k2tog, k1. (92 (97) (102) sts)

Following st pattern, cont straight until work measures 53 (54) (55)cm (21 (21¼) (21½)in) from cast on edge, ending on a WS row.

Neckline and shoulder shaping

Work each side of neck separately starting with left shoulder (see Note) as follows:

Row 1 (RS): Cast (bind) off 4 (5) (6) sts. Work as per pattern until there are 24 (25) (25) sts on the RN, turn, placing rem 64 (67) (71) sts on a st holder.

Row 2(WS): P2togtbl, work as per pattern to end. (23 (24) (24) sts)

Row 3: Cast (bind) off 5 sts, work as per pattern to end. (18 (19) (19) sts)

Row 4: P2togtbl, work as per pattern to end. (17 (18) (18) sts)

Rep above 2 rows twice more. (5 (6) (6) sts)

Cast (bind) off all 5 (6) (6) sts. Cut yarn, leaving enough tail to weave in end.

Return to sts on st holder, leave the centre 36 (37) (40) sts on st holder, transfer last 28 (30) (31) sts onto needle.

With RS facing, rejoin yarn to start shaping the right shoulder (see Note) as follows:

Next row (RS): K2tog, work as per pattern to end. (27 (29) (30) sts)

Next row (WS): Cast (bind) off 4 (5) (6) sts, work as per pattern to end. (23 (24) (24) sts)

Next row: K2tog, work as per pattern to end. (22 (23) (23) sts)

Next row: Cast (bind) off 5 sts, work as per pattern to end. (17 (18) (18) sts)

Rep above 2 rows two times more. (5 (6) (6) sts)

Cast (bind) off all 5 (6) (6) sts. Cut yarn, leaving enough tail to weave in end.

Sleeves (make 2)

Using 4mm (US 6) needles, cast on 65 sts.

Rib row 1 (RS): [K3, p2] to end of row.

Rib row 2 (WS): [K2, p3] to end of row.

Rep rib rows 1 and 2 until rib measures 7cm (2¾in).

Setup row 1 (RS): K1, M1L, k32 (32) (32), PM, p1, k to last st, M1R, k1. (67 (67) (67) sts)

Setup row 2 (WS): P to 1 st before marker, k1, SM, p to end.

Follow the st pattern repeat as established for back, and inc 1 st at the beg and end of every 6th row until there are 75 (79) (83) sts.

Continue working straight, maintaining st pattern until sleeve measures 39 (40) (41)cm (15¼ (15¾) (16)in) from cast on edge, ending on a WS row.

Upper sleeve shaping

Using dec instruction below, dec 1 st at beg and end of the next 4 alt rows while maintaining st pattern:

Dec row: K1, ssk, work as per st pattern to last 3 sts, k2tog, k1. (67 (71) (75) sts)

Work 1 row as per pattern.

Cast (bind) off. Cut yarn, leaving long enough tail to weave in end.

Assembly and finishing

Join front to back at both shoulders using mattress stitch (see Special Techniques).

NECKBAND:

With RS facing, using 3.25mm (US 3) circular needles or DPNs, starting from left shoulder seam pick up and knit 8 sts along the left neckline in the front, then knit the front 36 (37) (40) sts held on stitch holder, then pick up and knit 8 sts along the right neckline in front. Pick up and knit 3 sts to back of neck horizontal live st and then knit the back neck 40 (41, 44) sts held on stitch holder. Pick up and knit 3 sts to beginning of round. (98 (100, 106) sts)

Work in ss in the round for 7 rounds.

Cast (bind) off all sts.

Join cast (bound) off edge of a sleeve to armhole edge of body using mattress stitch. Rep for other sleeve.

Join the underarm and side seams also using mattress stitch.

Weave in ends.

Block for a professional finished look.

Useful Information

Abbreviations

alt: alternate

Bb: bobble

BOR: beginning of rnd/row

beg: beginning

C3B: cable 3 back. Slip next 2 st onto CN, leave CN to back of work, knit the next st from LN then knit 2 sts on CN

C4B: cable 4 back. Slip next 2 sts onto CN, hold CN to back of work, k2 from LN, then k2 from CN

C6B: cable 6 back. Slip next 3 sts onto CN, take CN to back of work, k3 from LN, then k3 from CN

C3F: cable 3 front. Slip next st onto CN, leave CN to front of work, knit the next 2 sts from LN then knit 1 st on the CN (cable is left leaning)

C6F: cable 6 front. Slip next 3 sts onto CN, take CN to front of work, k3, from LN, then k3 from CN

CC: contrast colour

CN: cable needle

cont: continue/continuing

dec: decrease/decreasing

DPN: double-pointed needles

DS: double stitch for German short rows

EOR: End of rnd/row

inc: increase/increasing

k: knit

k2tog: knit 2 sts together. For a right leaning decrease of 1 st

k2togtbl: knit 2 sts together through back loop

kfb: Knit front back. Knit into front and back of same stitch to increase by 1 stitch

kwise: knitwise. Insert your needle as if to knit

LN: left needle

LT: left twist. Slip next st onto CN, and hold in front of work, knit next st from LN then knit 1 st on CN

M1L: make 1 left. With LN tip, pick up horizontal bar linked to next st from front, knit into back loop. This results in new left leaning stitch

M1LP: make 1 purl left leaning. With left needle tip, pick up horizontal bar linked to the next stitch from the front, purl into the back loop

M1R: make 1 right. With LN tip, pick up horizontal bar linked to next st from back, knit into front loop. This results in new right leaning stitch

M1RP: Make 1 purl right leaning. With left needle tip, pick up horizontal bar linked to the next stitch from the back, purl into the front loop.

MC: main colour

p: purl

p2tog: purl 2 sts together

p2togtbl: purl 2 sts together through back loop. For a left leaning decrease of 1 stitch

Pfb: purl front and back. To increase by 1 st

PM: place marker on the needle

Pwise: purlwise. Insert your needle as if to purl

RCB: ribbed cable back. Slip next 4 sts onto CN, take CN to back of work, work next 4 sts from left needle as k1, p2, k1, then work 4 sts on CN as k1, p2, k1

RCF: ribbed cable front. Slip next 4 sts onto CN, take CN to front of work, work next 4 sts from left needle as k1, p2, k1, then work 4 sts on CN as k1, p2, k1

rem: remain/remaining

rep: repeat

RM: remove marker

RN: right needle

Rnd: round

RS: right side

RT: right twist. Slip next st onto CN and hold to back of work, k next st from left needle, then k st on CN

skpsso: slip next st knitwise. Knit next st, then pick up the slipped st and pass it over knitted one and off needle

sl1p: slip 1 st purlwise

SM: slip marker.

ss: stocking stitch. Knit on right side and purl on wrong side when worked flat

ssk: slip slip knit. Slip 1 st knitwise, slip next st knitwise, insert LN into front of 2 slipped sts from left to right and k them together. Left leaning decrease of 1 st

st(s): stitch(es)

WS: wrong side

wyif: with yarn in front

yfwd: yarn forward. Bring working yarn to front of work in between knitting needle tips

Yarn Weights

All of the yarns used in this book are from British rare breed sheep and some of them can be hard to find. Substitution suggestions are included in the Breed Directory, but you can also substitute with any yarn of the same weight. For instance, if the pattern uses a DK Romney, you can use any DK yarn.

Tension (Gauge)

Pattern tension, or gauge, is critical in making sure you get the specified fit when following a pattern. It's expressed in terms of the number of stitches and rows formed within a 10cm (4in) area, when working a specific stitch pattern using a specified needle size.

Before starting a new project, it's important to measure your tension and compare it against the pattern tension by knitting a swatch. If the tension you get is smaller than the specified tension, this means your knitting is loose. You'll need to reknit a swatch with a smaller needle size – until you're able to match the pattern tension. If your tension swatch has more stitches within the 10cm (4in) sample, then your knitting is tight, and you'll need to re-knit the swatch with a larger needle size.

With some garments where fit is not critical, such as scarves or shawls, knitting a swatch might not seem necessary. However, it's still important to create one to be sure of your yarn usage. Equally, if you've made a yarn substitution, you need to ensure that you like the result.

Tension information is key to working out any modifications you might want to make to a pattern. It can also be used to extract various measurements in the pattern that may be needed in order to check how a garment will fit.

To help with tension, particularly for smaller circles like sleeves, try knitting from the inside out (so that the outside of your knitting is on the purl side).

Care Tips for Working with Wool

Repetitive Strain Injury

Repetitive strain injury, which develops when you repeat the same action over and over, can be an issue for knitters. It often affects the wrists, hands, neck, and back. Poor posture, holding your needles too tight, or sitting for a long time can all contribute to the development of RSI, with signs including muscle tenderness, cramp, stiffness, a tingling sensation, numbness, or swelling.

Switching your knitting style or interchanging between techniques can help alleviate discomfort. Try English, underarm, continental, combination, or Portuguese styles to find a comfortable option and reduce strain on your shoulders, hands and wrists.

If the symptoms persist, it's advisable to give your knitting a rest until they disappear, otherwise you could exacerbate the situation, potentially causing long-term damage.

Moths

Common (webbing) clothes moths (*Tineola bisselliella*) love the warmth of centrally heated houses, meaning that most homes now have them. Upon hatching (over a four-to-ten-day period in summer and up to three weeks in colder weather) larvae emerge from their silk-spun tunnels at night to feed – creating the holes you'll find frustratingly often in your favourite items.

To protect against them, wash your garments and then store them in airtight bags or containers. Cedar oil or bags of dried lavender placed in your cupboards and wardrobes can also help.

If you experience a moth attack, soak the garment in cool water with wool soap overnight. Follow this with freezing them at -8°C for at least two weeks as this will kill all life stages. For clothes that can't be frozen, spraying pyethrin insecticides destroys the moths and doesn't leave toxic residues like many traditional chemicals. Moth traps – adhesive boxes which emit artificial pheromones to attract adult moths – are useful for breaking the breeding cycle and monitoring an infestation.

Washing Wool

It's best to soak wool overnight, as opposed to hand or machine-washing as you would other fabrics. Wool doesn't like abrasive action but giving it a good soak in wool detergent will dissolve any dirt. You can then give it a gentle rinse in the morning. Hand-washing wool products limits the risk of felting.

Woollen garments are best dried flat to avoid stretching. If you're short of space, you can spin them first to remove the excess water. The most important thing to remember is never to spin above 400rpm – otherwise you'll end up with a very small item.

Special Techniques

Mattress Stitch

This is the best way of sewing two knitted pieces together as it has a seamless look. You can use a tapestry/darning needle threaded with the same yarn or a substitute yarn of the same colour if your yarn is not strong enough.

Mattress stitch is worked with the right sides of both pieces facing upwards. There are three variations of mattress stitch:

Vertical Mattress Stitch

This is worked along the vertical side of the fabric, in the ditch next to the edge stitch and its adjacent stitch, where there are horizontal ladder bars corresponding to each row.

Lay the two knitted pieces flat, with the edges to be seamed adjoining. Begin by inserting the tapestry needle from back to front in-between your cast-on edge and the first row on the right-hand piece. Then insert your needle in the space between the cast on and first row of the left-hand piece from front to back then under two bars, pulling the thread through to the front in between rows two and three **(A)**.

Return to the right-hand piece and insert your needle in the same space from where the thread emerged previously (i.e. between cast on and row one) taking it under two bars and pulling the thread through to the front.

Next insert your needle into the same place in the left-hand piece from where the thread emerged in the previous step, taking it under two bars and pulling the thread through to the front. Then return to the right-hand piece, inserting your needle into the same space from where the thread emerged previously (i.e. between rows two and three) taking it under two bars and pulling the thread through to the front. Repeat these steps over and over **(B)**. Every few repeats, tighten the stitching by pulling on the thread **(C)**. Continue until the end of the seam.

Horizontal Mattress Stitch

Horizontal mattress stitch is used to join two cast (bound) off/on edges. An example is on the shoulder seam.

Lay both pieces flat with RS facing up and the cast (bound) off/on edges of both pieces adjoining. Begin by inserting your tapestry needle from back to front of piece A at the centre of the far end stitch. Pull the yarn through, leaving a bit of a tail to weave in later. Return to piece B by inserting the needle under the V of the far end stitch, pulling the thread through. Returning to piece A, insert your needle into the centre of the last stitch the thread came out of, then out of the centre of the next adjacent stitch, pulling the thread through. Next, return to piece B by inserting the needle under the next V stitch adjacent to the previously worked V. Repeat these steps, working on every stitch of each piece. Every few repeats, tighten the stitching by pulling the yarn. Continue until all the stitches are done.

Horizontal to Vertical Stitch

This is used to join cast-off stitches to rows. An example is when sewing the top of a sleeve to an armhole edge. This is a situation where you work one side as if it's a horizontal mattress stitch and the other side as a vertical mattress. Since there are usually more rows per inch (2.5cm) than stitches, occasionally you will need to pick up two horizontal ladder bars on the piece with rows for every stitch on the cast-off piece.

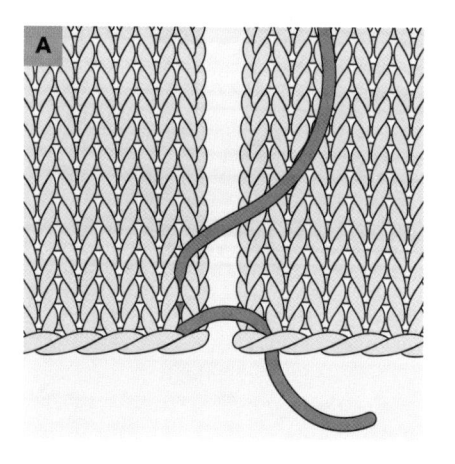

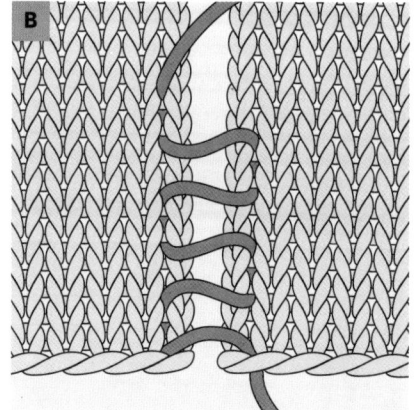

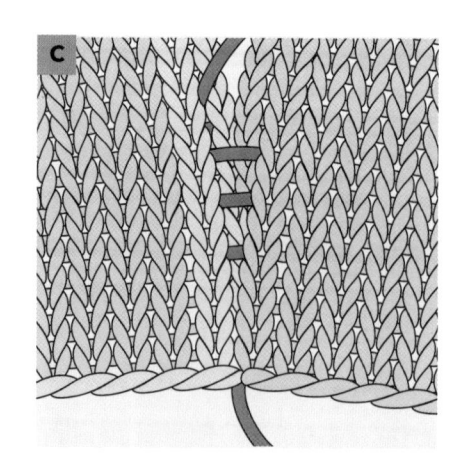

Joining Chain Stitch

This is a decorative way to join two panels. Start by threading a darning needle with a long length of yarn to match your garment.

Step 1: take the two panels to be joined and lay them on top of each other, WS facing each other. Pull your yarn through the bottom stitch to secure the panels at the base **(D)**.

Step 2: thread your needle under the stitch you've created at the base, then pull it through the bottom loops of the next stitches on the right and left panels **(E)**.

Step 3: go under the bar of the stitch just created and repeat to create the joined seam **(F)**.

German Short Rows

Worked part way along the row to add extra height in a specific area of a knit. There are many uses for short rows, such as shaping shoulders or for decorative design effect. German short rows is one of several techniques available and is used in a few of the book's patterns because of its simplicity and seamlessness.

Work your row as specified in the pattern, turning the work over so that the wrong side is now facing up. With your yarn in front, slip your next stitch from LN to RN **(G)**, taking the working yarn from the front of your work to the back over RN while tugging the yarn so that the two legs of the stitch below are raised and wrap over RN **(H)**. This stitch is referred to as a "double stitch" (DS). Then, proceed to work as per the instructions. The double stitch is always worked as one stitch **(I)**.

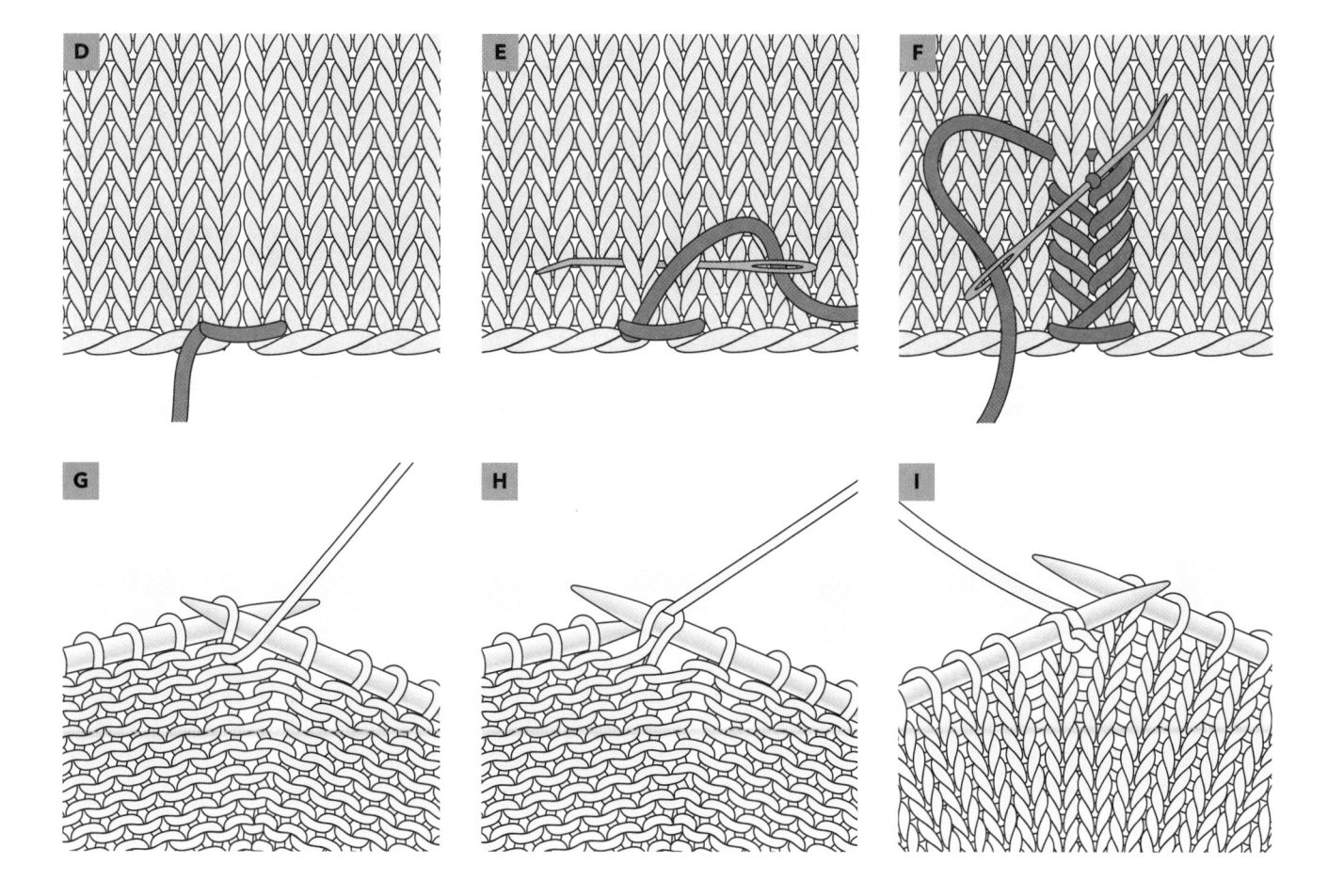

Special Techniques • 137

Four-stitch Buttonhole

This method creates a clean firm edged buttonhole in one row. Work to start point where buttonhole is to be made

Step 1: Wrap next stitch as follows:

   a. Take yarn to opposite side of work in between needles

   b. Slip next stitch from left to right needle,

   c. Take yarn back to original side of work in between needles **(A)**.

Step 2: Slip next stitch from left to right needle, then pick up previous slipped stitch on right needle and pass over last slipped stitch and off needle similar to cast (bind) off.

Step 3: Rep step 2 three times more.

Step 4: Slip last stitch back from right to left needle and then turn work so that WS is facing you.

Step 5: Cast on 5 stitches using cable cast on method **(B)**. Turn work so that RS is facing you.

Step 6: If next stitch on left needle is a knit then with yarn in back slip last cast on stitch from right needle to left needle, then k2tog **(C)**. If next stitch on left needle is a purl then with yarn in front, slip last cast on stitch from right needle to left, then p2tog.

Three-needle Cast (Bind) off

This method creates a horizontal join between two knitted pieces without having to cast (bind) off each piece individually then sew them together. It's used to join two edges with live stitches and provides stability on the join. This method is useful for places such as shoulder seams or a back neck collar.

You need three needles: one to hold one set of live stitches on piece A, another to hold the second set of live stitches on piece B and a third to use as your working needle.

Step 1: Transfer the stitches from their holders onto knitting needles. With the right sides of the work facing each other and the two needles pointing in the same direction, hold the needles in your left hand **(D)**.

Step 2: With your third needle, work into the back of the first stitch on the front needle, and then into the front of the first stitch on the back needle, then knit the two stitches together **(E)**.

Repeat this so that there are two stitches on the third needle and then start to cast (bind) off **(F)**, by taking the first stitch and passing it over the second stitch and off the needle.

Step 3: Repeat step 2 until all the stitches on the two left needles are worked in, and only one stitch is left on the right needle. Fasten off the yarn as you would for normal cast (bind) off.

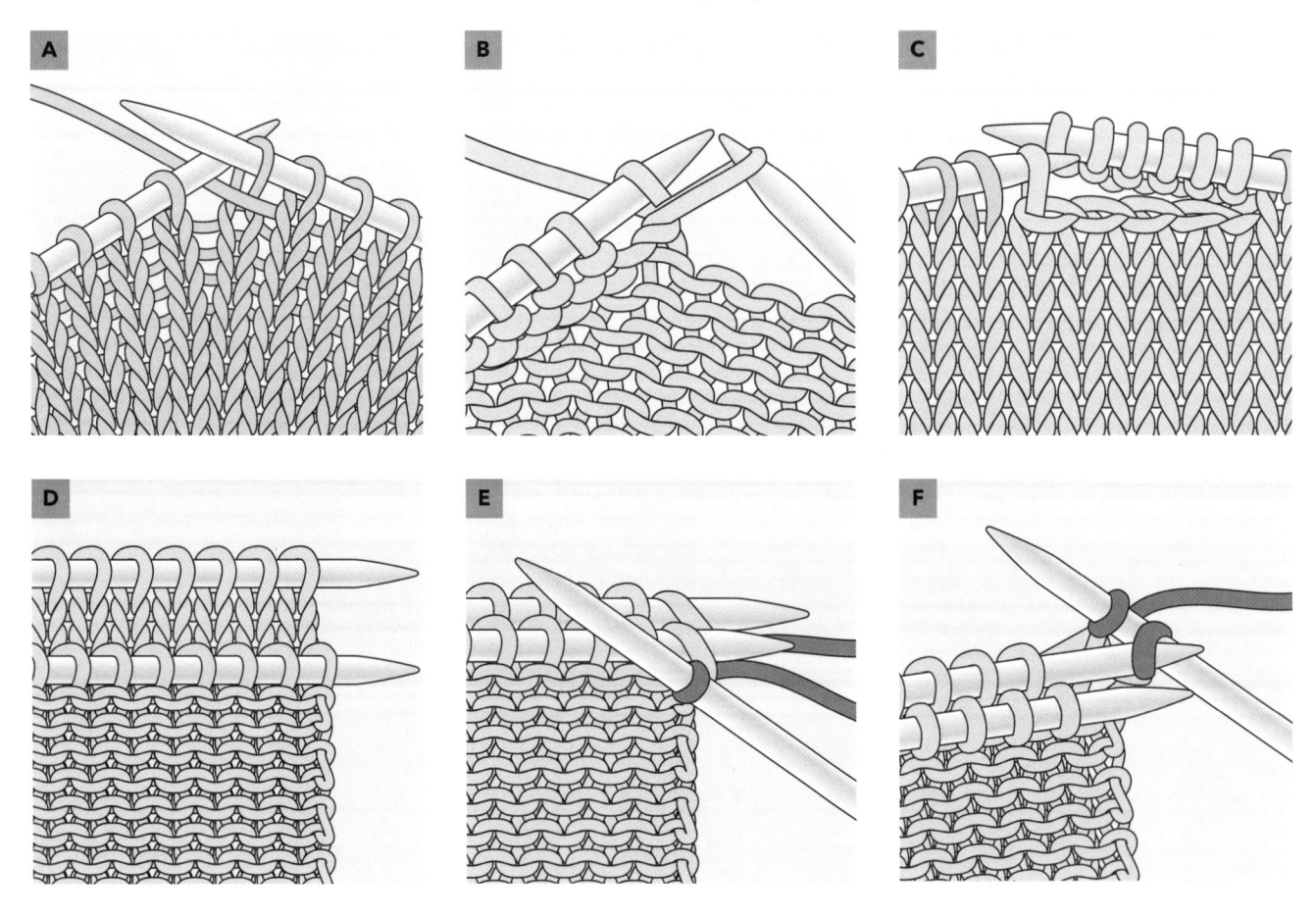

138 · Special Techniques

Bobble (Bb)

Step 1: Work to the point at which you want to create a bobble. Inc next st into 4 sts by knitting into front and back **(G)** of st twice without sliding it off left needle until 4th st **(H)**. Turn work.

Step 2: P4. Turn work.

Step 3: Sl1p, k2, sl1p **(I)**. Turn work.

Step 4: Dec 4 sts into 2 by: p2tog twice **(J)**. Turn work.

Step 5: K2tog **(K)**. Continue with pattern.

Blocking

Blocking is an essential step in finishing a knitted piece. It dramatically enhances the look of the garment by evening-out stitch irregularities and restoring shape.

Wet Blocking

Soak the item in a basin of lukewarm water with a small amount of wool wash for about 20 minutes, making sure it's thoroughly wet. Rinse if required, then drain the water and gently squeeze the piece. Roll your handknit in dry towels to remove excess moisture – do not twist or wring. Shape the piece right side up on a flat padded surface, like blocking pads, using pins or blocking wires as necessary.

Steam Blocking

Applying steam to the fabric and saturating it with moisture relaxes the stitching, making it easier to handle the knit during the seaming process. You can use a steam iron or a clothes steamer.

This method can be used for individually knitted pieces that will later be seamed together. The advantage is that one can apply a degree of gentle manipulation to even up slightly different sizes if needed.

Begin by placing the dry knitted piece on a blocking pad, a stack of towels, or an ironing board. Pin it to the desired measurements using rust-proof pins (such as T-pins) or blocking wires if desired.

Hold the steam iron or steamer about an inch above the knit, moving it slowly to make sure the steam penetrates the fabric. Never place the iron directly on the garment or you'll burn it.

NOTE: Always check the label on the yarn for the care of the fibre.

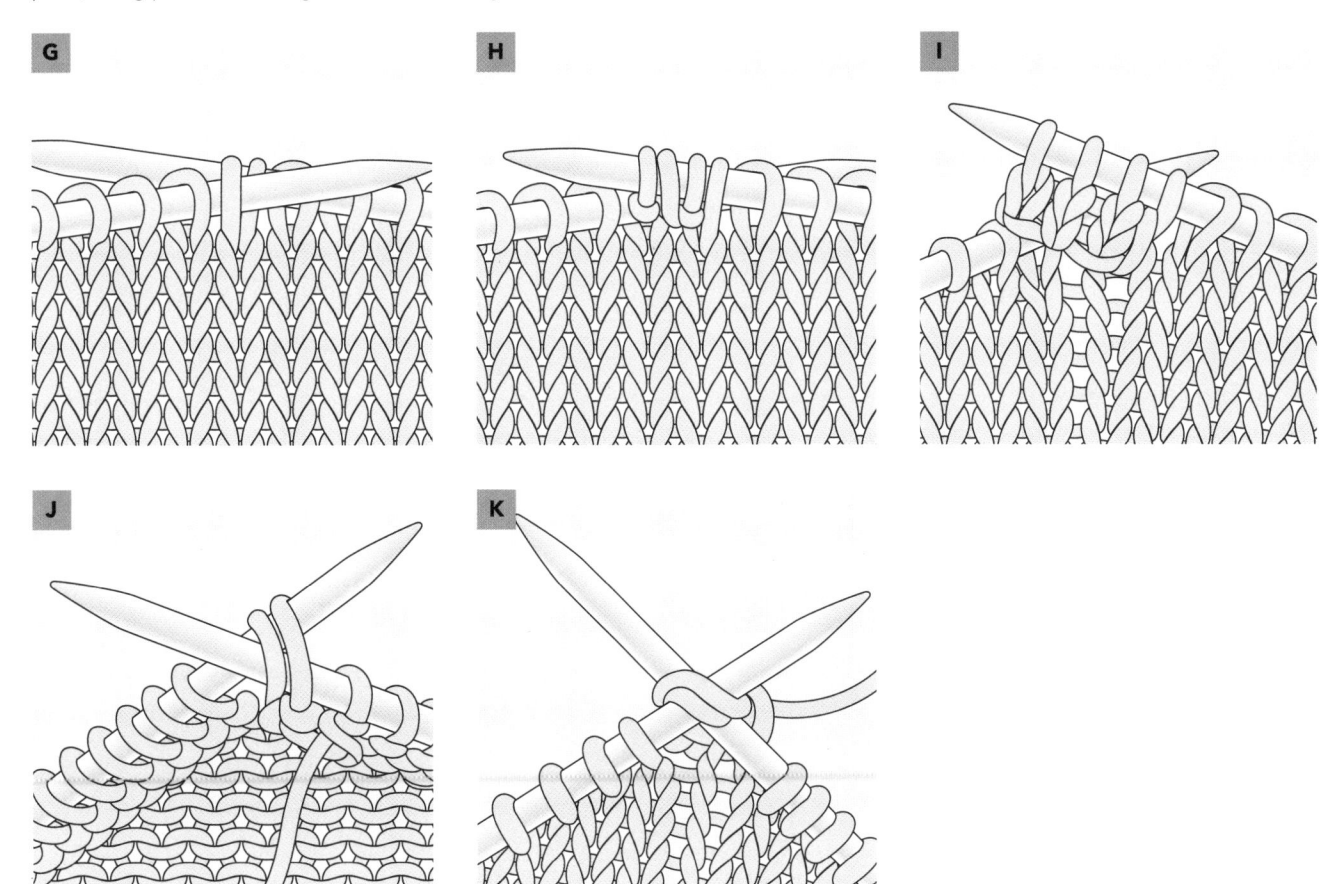

Sourcing Guide

Black Welsh Mountain

Blacker Yarns (UK) – blackeryarns.co.uk

SortTraeStudio (UK) – etsy.com/shop/SortTraeStudio

The Ross Farm Yarn (USA) – therossfarm.com

Bluefaced Leicester

Barefaced Knits (UK) – jostorieknits.com

Chimera (UK) – riverknits.co.uk

Laura's Loom (UK) – laurasloom.co.uk

McIntosh (UK) – shop.knitmcintosh.com

Wensleydale Longwool Sheep Shop (UK) – wensleydalelongwool.co.uk

West Yorkshire Spinners (UK) – wyspinners.com

World of Wool (UK) – worldofwool.co.uk

Jagger Spun (USA) – jaggeryarn.com

Juniper Moon Farm (USA) – junipermoonfarmyarn.com

Sally Ridgway (AUS) – sallyridgway.com.au

Border Leicester

Doulton Border Leicester Yarn (UK) – doultonborderleicesteryarn.com

Bare Naked Wools (USA) – barenakedwools.com

Feindt Family Farm (USA) – etsy.com/shop/feindtfamilyfarm

Boreray

Orkney Boreray (UK) – orkneyboreray.com

Sheepfold (UK) – sheepfold.co.uk

Wychwood Spinner (UK) – etsy.com/uk/shop/WychwoodSpinner

British Milk sheep

Ossian Knitwear (UK) – ossianknitwear.co.uk

Castlemilk Moorit

Caithness Yarns (UK) – caithnessyarns.com

Foxbank Farm (UK) – etsy.com/uk/shop/Foxbankfarm

Laura's Loom (UK) – laurasloom.co.uk

The Lost Sheep Company (UK) – thelostsheepcompany.co.uk (see also etsy.com/uk/shop/thelostsheepcompany)

The Wool Library (UK) – thewoollibrary.uk

Cheviot

Caithness Yarns (UK) – caithnessyarns.com

Heatherlea Black Cheviot (UK) – blackcheviot.com

SortTraeStudio (UK) – etsy.com/shop/SortTraeStudio

The Wool Library (UK) – thewoollibrary.uk

Junction Fiber Mill (USA) – junctionfibermill.com

Cotswold

Brentford Fox Yarns (UK) – brentfoxyarns.sumupstore.com

Wychwood Spinner (UK) – etsy.com/uk/shop/WychwoodSpinner

Shaggy Bear Farms (USA) – shaggybearfarms.com

Dorset Down

Gutchpool Farm (UK) – gutchpool.com

Rampisham Hill Farm (UK) – rampishamhillfarm.co.uk

Greyface Dartmoor

Lily Warne Wool (UK) – lilywarnewool.co.uk

Hampshire Down

Halifax Spinning Mill (UK) – halifaxspinningcompany.co.uk

The Grey Sheep Co. (UK) – thegreysheep.co.uk

Hebridean

Daughter of a Shepherd (UK) – daughterofashepherd.com

Garthenor Organic Yarns (UK) – garthenor.com

The Birlinn Yarn Company (UK) – birlinnyarn.co.uk

The Woolly Thistle (UK) – thewoollythistle.com

Herdwick

Crookabeck Farm (UK) – crookabeck.co.uk

Helder-Herdwyck Farm (USA) – helderherdwyckfarm.com

Jacob

Blacker Yarns (UK) – blackeryarns.co.uk

Brent Fox Yarns (UK) – brentfox.co.uk

The Lost Sheep Company (UK) – thelostsheepcompany.co.uk (see also etsy.com/uk/shop/thelostsheepcompany)

West Yorkshire Spinners (UK) – wyspinners.com

Junction Fiber Mill (USA) – junctionfibermill.com

The Ross Farm (USA) – therossfarm.com

Wool Chambers (AUS) – etsy.com/shop/WoolChambers

Leicester Longwool
Flock & Skien (UK) – 4faa78-4.myshopify.com
Pen-y-Lan Fibre Flock (UK) – folksy.com/shops/penylanfibreflock
River Knits (UK) – riverknits.co.uk
The Ross Farm (USA) – therossfarm.com

Llanwenog
Welsh Fibre Company (UK) – welshfibrecompany.com

Lleyn
Brent Fox Yarns (UK) – brentfox.co.uk
Halifax Spinning Mill (UK) – halifaxspinningcompany.co.uk
The Raw Wool Company (UK) – rawwoolcompany.co.uk

Manx Loaghtan
Blacker Yarns (UK) – blackeryarns.co.uk
Manx J Produce (UK) – store.manxloaghtanproduce.com
Sheepfold (UK) – sheepfold.co.uk

Masham
By Laxtons (UK) – bylaxtons.co.uk
The Rushlade Wool Company (UK) – rushladewool.co.uk

Norfolk Horn
Fibreworkshop (UK) – fibreworkshop.co.uk

North Ronaldsay
Blacker Yarns (UK) – blackeryarns.co.uk
Sheepfold (UK) – sheepfold.co.uk
Wool Chambers (AUS) – etsy.com/shop/WoolChambers

Oxford Down
Brent Fox Yarns (UK) – brentfox.co.uk
Wychwood Spinner (UK) – etsy.com/uk/shop/WychwoodSpinner

Portland
Armscote Manor (UK) – armscotemanor.co.uk
Sheepfold (UK) – sheepfold.co.uk
The Woven Briar (UK) – thewovenbriar.co.uk

Romney
By Laxtons (UK) – bylaxtons.co.uk
Fernhill Fibre (UK) – fernhillfibre.co.uk
John Arbon (UK) – jarbon.com
Romany Marsh Wools (UK) – romneymarshwools.co.uk
Junction Fiber Mill (USA) – junctionfibermill.com
The Fibre Company (USA) – thefibreco.com

Ryeland
Halifax Spinning Mill (UK) – halifaxspinningcompany.co.uk
Nurture From Nature (UK) – nurturefromnature.co.uk

Shropshire
Flock of Ages (UK) – flockofages.co.uk
Wool on the Exe (UK) – woolontheexe.com
Shaggy Bear Farms (USA) – shaggybearfarms.com

Soay
Parva Brook (UK) – parvabrook.com
Wychwood Spinner (UK) – etsy.com/uk/shop/WychwoodSpinner
Still River Mill (USA) – stillrivermill.com

Southdown
WOOL SHrED (UK) – woolshred.co.uk

Teeswater
The Wool Library (UK) – thewoollibrary.uk

Wensleydale
Home Farm Wensleydales (UK) – homefarmwensleydales.com
Raw Wool company (UK) – rawwoolcompany.co.uk
Shear Wensleydale (UK) – shearwensleydale.com
Wensleydale Longwool Sheep Shop (UK) – wensleydalelongwool.co.uk

About the Authors

Justine Lee

Justine is a knitwear designer who has spent many years working in the fashion industry. After completing a Masters' degree in sustainable textiles she created Ossian Knitwear, a brand dedicated to promoting the diversity of British wool and supporting sheep farmers, while also being gentle on the environment. She works from her studio in West London.

Acknowledgements

To Tom Lee, my husband, for his wonderful sheep portraits which make this book so special. I would also like to thank Jess for having a belief in me that I did not have myself and without whom this book would not have existed.

My gratitude also goes to Suzanne Strachan for her pattern writing skills and for finding sample knitters from her knitting group, 'Knit and Pearl' including Catherine Withycombe, Catherine Dolan, Paula Fitzgerald, and Fiona Grundy. And to Nick Farrell for his beautiful lino print.

For expert sheep advice I would like to thank Tom Blunt from the Rare Breed Survival trust, Fiona Parker from the National Sheep Association, Louisa Knapp from British Wool, David Wilkins from Rampisham Mill, and Frank Langrish.

I must also thank the following farmers who donated yarn for the projects. It was much appreciated. Armscote Manor, the Black Cheviot Company, Doulton Border Leicester, and the West Yorkshire Spinners.

Jess Morency

Jess is a feature writer and novelist, currently doing a PhD in Creative Writing. Based in Dorset, she's a staunch supporter of artisan crafts and an experienced dressmaker. To her eternal disappointment she cannot knit; despite many attempts at trying to learn.

Acknowledgements

My first thanks go to Justine for knitting me the most beautiful heritage cardigan ('Mouse' grey, made from the North Country Cheviot) which was the catalyst for this project.

I'd also like to thank, for expert input on all things sheep and history, plus a bit of helpful proof reading: Malcolm Dampier, Mary Doble, David Johnstone, Declan McCarthy, Sara Milne, Jennifer Mole, and Malcolm Thompson. Plus my husband, Pete, for my author photo, and The Dorset Guild of Weavers, Dyers and Spinners: for putting the call out when we needed some knitters. And to Caitlin Atkinson for answering the call.

Many thanks as well to my children, Imani and Jai Thompson, and to Imogen Gray for modelling the garments so beautifully – despite the Dartmoor cold! To Peter Chillingworth for help with the smugglers' illustration and Mike Baldwin for his wonderful Minchinhampton photo.

We would both like to thank the team at David & Charles for commissioning this book. Everyone was so enthusiastic, right from the start, which we really appreciated. Special thanks go to Sarah Callard, Victoria Allen, Lucy Ridley and Sophie Seager, as well as Clare Hunt, Sarah Rowntree, Jason Jenkins, Joelle Wheelwright, Hannah Maltby, and Jane Simmonds.

Index

abbreviations 134
armhole shaping 66, 132-3

ball winders (yarn winders) 56
Black Welsh Mountain 24, 55, 128-33, 140
black-faced hornless 11
blocking 139
Bluefaced Leicester (BFL) 34, 55, 84-91, 92-9, 140
bobble stitches 55, 112-19, 139
Border Leicester 35, 55, 74-83, 140
Boreray 23, 25, 140
British Milk Sheep 36, 140
buttonhole, four-stitch 138

cable 55, 68-73, 92-9, 112-19
cakes (wool balls) 56
cardigan, Tara 55, 92-9
cashmere 6, 18-19, 25, 34
Castlemilk Moorit 3, 26, 55, 92-9, 140
chain stitch, joining 137
Cheviot 3, 44, 55, 61, 74-83, 120-7, 140
Cotswold 3, 37, 140
cuff ribs 89

Dorset Down 3, 45, 140
down and shortwool breeds 22, 23, 44-53, 61
 see also specific breeds

embroidery 79-83

Fair Isle knitting
 Carril Fair Isle jumper 55, 84-91
 Orla paisley intarsia sweater 55, 120-7
farming, organic/regenerative 18-19
fast fashion 19

German short rows 137
gilet, Cola 55, 68-73
Greyface Dartmoor 3, 38, 140

Hampshire Down 3, 46, 140
hank winders 56
Hat, Atha Checkered 55, 100-5
Hebridean 3, 27, 140
Herdwick 3, 28, 140
horizontal to vertical stitch 136

intarsia 55, 120-7

Jacob 29, 55, 100-5, 140
joining, chain stitch 137
jumpers
 Carril Fair Isle 55, 84-91
 Furgus unisex 55, 62-7
 see also sweaters

Leicester Longwool 23, 39, 55, 68-73, 141
Llanwenog 47, 141
Lleyn 48, 141
longwool breeds 22, 23, 34-43, 61
 see also specific breeds

Manx Loaghtan 3, 30, 141
Masham 40, 141
materials 56-7
mattress stitch 136
merino 6, 14, 16, 18-19, 22, 41, 51
moths 135
mouflon 8-11, 33

neckbands, jumper 67
necks
 cardigans 96-8
 jumpers 66-7, 88
 sweaters 79, 110-11, 125, 133
 trim 111
needles
 cable 59
 circular 58-9
 double-pointed 58
 latch 59
 straight 57
 tapestry/darning 59
Norfolk Horn 3, 49, 141
North Ronaldsay 3, 23, 31, 141

Oxford Down 3, 50, 141

paisley 55, 112-19, 120-7
Portland 32, 55, 112-19, 141
primitive breeds 22-33, 61
 see also specific breeds
projects 54-133

raglan sleeves 78-9, 110-11
repetitive strain injury (RSI) 135
Romney 3, 16, 23, 41, 55, 106-11, 141
row counters 59
Ryeland 3, 23, 51, 141

shawl, Malvina 55, 112-19

sheep
 breed directory 20-53
 domestication 9
 evolution 11
 history 8-15
 land and dietary changes 12
 shearing 16
 welfare 18
 see also specific breeds
sheep societies 61
Shetland 3, 11, 16, 22, 26, 44, 106-8
shoulders 66-7, 72-3, 96-8, 133
Shropshire 3, 52, 141
sizing 56-7, 59
sleeves 78-9
 cardigans 98
 jumpers 67, 88-9, 91
 raglan 78-9, 110-11
 sweaters 78-9, 124, 133
slow fashion 19
Soay 3, 6, 10, 33, 141
South Down 53, 141
spinning 60
sustainability 6, 18-19, 57-8
sweaters
 Moina 55, 74-83
 Orla paisley intarsia 55, 120-7
 Semo 55, 106-11
 Ullin 55, 128-33
 see also jumpers
synthetic fibres 15

Teeswater 23, 42, 141
tension (gauge) 59, 135
terminology 22
three-needle cast (bind) off 138
tools 56-7

unisex designs, jumpers 55, 62-7

washing wool 60, 135
waste 6
Wensleydale 43, 55, 62-7, 141
white-faced hornless 11, 23
Wiltshire 6
wool
 campaign for 15
 feel 61
 rise and fall of 10-15
 variation 60
 versatility 16
 working with 60-1, 135

yarn weights 135
yokes 88, 90, 124-5

Index • 143

A DAVID AND CHARLES BOOK
© David and Charles, Ltd 2025

David and Charles is an imprint of David and Charles, Ltd
Suite A, Tourism House, Pynes Hill, Exeter, EX2 5WS

Text and Designs © Justine Lee and Jess Morency 2025
Layout and Photography © David and Charles, Ltd 2025
See image credits for exceptions.

First published in the UK and USA in 2025

Justine Lee and Jess Morency have asserted their right to be identified as authors of this work in accordance with the Copyright, Designs and Patents Act, 1988.

All rights reserved. No part of this publication may be reproduced in any form or by any means, electronic or mechanical, by photocopying, recording or otherwise, without prior permission in writing from the publisher.

No part of this book may be used or reproduced in any manner for the purpose of training artificial intelligence technologies or systems without permission from David and Charles Ltd.

Readers are permitted to reproduce any of the designs in this book for their personal use and without the prior permission of the publisher. However, the designs in this book are copyright and must not be reproduced for resale.

The author and publisher have made every effort to ensure that all the instructions in the book are accurate and safe, and therefore cannot accept liability for any resulting injury, damage or loss to persons or property, however it may arise.

Names of manufacturers and product ranges are provided for the information of readers, with no intention to infringe copyright or trademarks.

A catalogue record for this book is available from the British Library.

ISBN-13: 9781446315453 hardback
ISBN-13: 9781446315477 EPUB

This book has been printed on paper from approved suppliers and made from pulp from sustainable sources.

FSC® C136333 MIX Paper | Supporting responsible forestry

Printed in China through Asia Pacific Offset for:
David and Charles, Ltd
Suite A, Tourism House, Pynes Hill, Exeter, EX2 5WS

10 9 8 7 6 5 4 3 2 1

Publishing Director: Ame Verso
Senior Commissioning Editor: Sarah Callard
Publishing Manager: Jeni Chown
Editor: Victoria Allen
Project Editors: Jane Simmonds and Clare Hunt
Technical Editor: Hannah Maltby
Lead Designer: Sam Staddon
Designers: Lucy Ridley and Joelle Wheelwright
Pre-press Designer: Susan Reansbury
Illustrations: Justine Lee
Technique Illustrations: Matilda Smith and Kuo Kang Cheng
Art Direction: Sarah Rowntree
Photography: Jason Jenkins
Production Manager: Beverley Richardson

Image credits
p 4-5, 7, 10, 13, 17, 23, 62, 68, 74, 84, 92, 100, 112, 120, 128: photos © Tom Lee (www. tomlee.gallery)
p12: Minchinhampton Church from Ram Inn © Mike Baldwin
p20: linocut print © Nick Farrell (nfarrgone@virginmedia.com)

David and Charles publishes high-quality books on a wide range of subjects. For more information visit www.davidandcharles.com.

Share your makes with us on social media using #dandcbooks and follow us on Facebook and Instagram by searching for @dandcbooks.

Layout of the digital edition of this book may vary depending on reader hardware and display settings.

Thanks to

The Little Knitting Company (thelittleknittingcompany.co.uk) for supplying the tools and materials shown on pages 56-59.

Butterwalk in Totnes for supplying the wonderful clothing made by NAAiNAAi (naainaai.co.uk) shown on pages 71, 87, and 131.

Rugglestone Inn (rugglestoneinn.co.uk) for kindly allowing us to shoot in front of their establishment.

Lotta (lottafromstockholm.co.uk) for supplying the lace-up boots shown on pages 71 and 77.

Further reading

A Short History of the World According to Sheep by Sally Coulthard

Much Ado About Mutton by Bob Kennard

The Price of Fast Fashion and the Future of Clothes by Dana Thomas

The Sheep's Tale by John Lewis-Stempel